EXPLORERS
and
EXPLORATION

VOLUME 2

THE GOLDEN AGE OF EXPLORATION

Paul Brewer

Grolier Educational

SHERMAN TURNPIKE, DANBURY, CONNECTICUT 06816

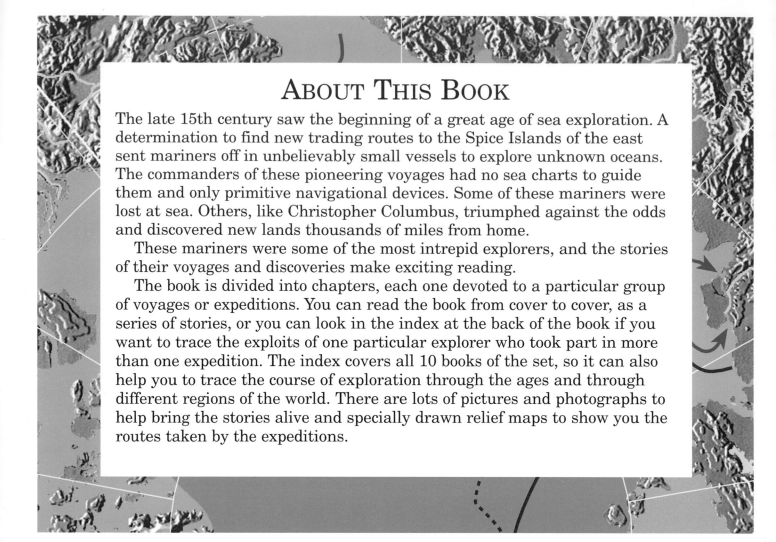

ABOUT THIS BOOK

The late 15th century saw the beginning of a great age of sea exploration. A determination to find new trading routes to the Spice Islands of the east sent mariners off in unbelievably small vessels to explore unknown oceans. The commanders of these pioneering voyages had no sea charts to guide them and only primitive navigational devices. Some of these mariners were lost at sea. Others, like Christopher Columbus, triumphed against the odds and discovered new lands thousands of miles from home.

These mariners were some of the most intrepid explorers, and the stories of their voyages and discoveries make exciting reading.

The book is divided into chapters, each one devoted to a particular group of voyages or expeditions. You can read the book from cover to cover, as a series of stories, or you can look in the index at the back of the book if you want to trace the exploits of one particular explorer who took part in more than one expedition. The index covers all 10 books of the set, so it can also help you to trace the course of exploration through the ages and through different regions of the world. There are lots of pictures and photographs to help bring the stories alive and specially drawn relief maps to show you the routes taken by the expeditions.

Published 1998 by Grolier Educational
Sherman Turnpike
Danbury, Connecticut 06816

© 1998 Brown Partworks Ltd

Set ISBN: 0-7172-9135-9
Volume ISBN: 0-7172-9137-5

Cover picture: AKG, London

For information address the publisher:
Grolier Educational, Sherman Turnpike, Danbury, Connecticut 06816

Library of Congress Cataloging-in-Publication Data
Grolier student library of explorers and exploration
p.cm.—Includes indexes.—Contents: vol.1. The earliest explorers—vol.2. The golden age of exploration—vol.3. Europe's imperial adventurers—vol.4. Scientists and explorers—vol.5. Latin America—vol.6. North America—vol.7. Australasia and Asia—vol.8. Africa and Arabia—vol.9. Polar explorers—vol.10. Space and underwater.

1. Discoveries in geography—Juvenile literature. 2. Explorers—Juvenile literature. [1. Discoveries in geography. 2. Explorers.] I. Grolier Educational Corporation.
G175.G75 1997   97-27683
910.9—dc.21   CIP
                                                            AC

For Brown Partworks Ltd
Editor: Shona Grimbly
Designers: Joan Curtis and Paul Griffin
Picture research: Brigitte Arora
Maps: David Heidenstam
Text editor: Matthew Turner

Printed in Singapore

CONTENTS

The Golden Age of Exploration

Cordaiy Photo Library Ltd/Corbis

THE VOYAGES
OF
COLUMBUS

Christopher Columbus's "discovery" of America is one of the world's most famous stories of exploration. Yet what Columbus set out to discover was a new sea route to Asia, and when he made landfall, he thought he was in the Indies. When Columbus reached—as he believed—a small island off the coast of Asia on October 12, 1492, he was in fact in the Bahamas, a chain of islands off Florida's Atlantic coast. He was 8,500 miles (13,600 km) east of his goal.

How could such a monumental error happen? To answer that, it is necessary to look at Columbus's life and understand the times he lived in.

HUMBLE BEGINNINGS

Christopher Columbus was born in 1451 in Genoa, Italy. His father Domenico worked as a weaver and seems to have been a prosperous one, since he held a

"Land! Land!" When the lookout on the Pinta (below right) sighted land in the early hours of October 12, 1492, Columbus believed he had reached Asia. Instead he had discovered the Bahamas (below) in the

Caribbean Sea. The fleet dropped anchor in calm waters, and the next morning Columbus launched a longboat and landed on an island at noon. He named the island San Salvador.

minor public office in a city ruled by men of wealth. Christopher's first sea voyage was in 1474 or 1475, at the age of 23 or 24, to the island of Chios in the Aegean Sea, which was then ruled by Genoa.

Columbus fell in love with the seafarer's life. He made several voyages—to Madeira, along the African coast, and across the Mediterranean. There is a possibly exaggerated report that in 1476, the ship he was on was sunk in a battle with a French and Portuguese pirate fleet. With the support of an oar he swam the six miles (10 km) to the shore. Even

Metropolitan Museum of Art, N.Y./AKG, London

Christopher Columbus (above) went to sea as a young man and became a master mariner in 1480.

if this exploit were fiction, Columbus did learn to sail the hard way—serving under tough taskmasters on small ships in rough seas.

THE SPICE TRADE

Columbus's home town of Genoa, along with Pisa and Venice, was one of the three great seaports of medieval Italy. Genoese merchants traded many goods—grain, oil, wine, salt, wool, and lead. But they made the most money from trading in spices, the most valuable being black pepper, cinnamon, nutmeg, and cloves.

The spice trade originated in Marco Polo's time, in the 13th century, when the spices were transported overland by caravan from the Far East. By the 15th century the overland route had given way to shipping routes, and the spices now came to Europe mainly by sea.

From the so-called Spice Islands of what is now Indonesia Chinese merchants shipped the spices to Malacca on the west coast of Malaya. From there

Mary Evans Picture Library

Mary Evans Picture Library

Muslim traders carried the spices by sea to western India, and then shipped them to Egypt or to the mouth of the Euphrates River in the Persian Gulf. Then they were taken overland to ports on the Mediterranean coast.

At every stage in the journey the spices were sold on, so by the time they reached Europe, at least four people had added to the price originally paid to the farmer in Indonesia. Clearly, if an enterprising merchant discovered a direct route to the Far East, he could undercut the normal prices being charged and at the same time make a huge profit.

COLUMBUS'S CALCULATIONS

At some time in the 1470s Columbus moved to Lisbon in Portugal, where there was a large Genoese community that included his brother Bartholomew.

There, Columbus became familiar with a theory about the size of the Earth. For many years educated Europeans had known that they lived on a globe: what was open to question was its size.

On a voyage along the coast of West Africa, Columbus took many sightings of the sun's altitude. He knew of an Arabic calculation of a degree of latitude at the Equator being equal to 56⅔ miles (90 km)—it is in fact nearly 60 miles (96 km) —but was unaware that this used the Arabic mile, which was longer than that in use in Europe.

By selecting facts to suit his case from ancient and medieval writers, Columbus decided that Asia stretched farther eastward than most scholars believed and that the globe was smaller than any previous geographer had calculated. The effect of all these calculations was to make

Columbus first tried to sell his grand idea of sailing west to Asia to King John II of Portugal, but he was turned down. He then approached King Ferdinand and Queen Isabella of Spain, who set up a royal commission at Salamanca to examine Columbus's proposals (above).

Mary Evans Picture Library

MARTIN BEHAIM AND THE GLOBE

Martin Behaim of Nuremburg was one of four important German writers who systematically created a science of geography. He lived in the late 15th century and is best remembered as the maker of the earliest globe still in existence.

Behaim's globe shows the world as the medieval mind pictured it: without the Americas, and with Asia stretching as far east as longitude 234°. Behaim outlined the shapes of the continents by hand on vellum, using colored inks, as in the charts used by pilots at sea in the 15th century.

the Ocean (in Columbus's time it was believed there was only one) some 2,400 miles (3,850 km) wide.

In 1484 Columbus presented a plan to King John II of Portugal. He wanted the king to pay for a ship to sail west across the Ocean to find a new trade route to Asia. King John turned him down. The following year Columbus began what would prove to be a six-year struggle to persuade the Spanish monarchs, Ferdinand and Isabella, to finance him.

Ferdinand and Isabella appointed a royal commission of experts to study Columbus's theories and report on them. The commission correctly thought he had miscalculated the size of the globe. In January 1492, however, he finally won approval for his plan. The size of the expedition—three ships—was so small that if it was a failure it would have cost the Spanish treasury little.

THE FIRST VOYAGE

Columbus knew from his voyage down the west coast of Africa that the prevailing wind around latitude 28° North blew from the northeast, ideal for a westerly voyage. So on August 3, 1492, he left Palos near Seville in Spain for the Canaries. From these Spanish-controlled islands he set sail on September 6 on a westward course across the Ocean.

AKG, London

Above: Columbus's first expedition sets off from Palos, a small port in the southwest of Spain.

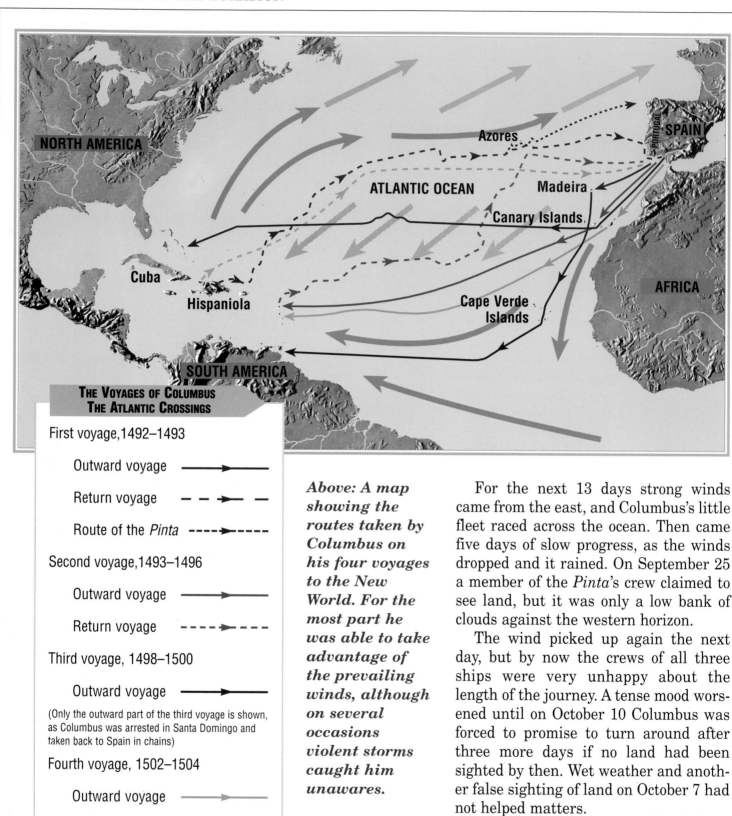

NORTH AMERICA

ATLANTIC OCEAN

Azores

Madeira

Canary Islands

SPAIN

PORTUGAL

AFRICA

Cuba

Hispaniola

Cape Verde
Islands

SOUTH AMERICA

THE VOYAGES OF COLUMBUS
THE ATLANTIC CROSSINGS

First voyage, 1492–1493

Outward voyage	⟶
Return voyage	– – ➤ –
Route of the *Pinta*	---- ➤ ----

Second voyage, 1493–1496

| Outward voyage | ⟶ |
| Return voyage | ---- ➤ ---- |

Third voyage, 1498–1500

| Outward voyage | ⟶ |

(Only the outward part of the third voyage is shown, as Columbus was arrested in Santo Domingo and taken back to Spain in chains)

Fourth voyage, 1502–1504

| Outward voyage | ⟶ |
| Return voyage | ---- ➤ ---- |

| Prevailing winds | ⟶ |
| Prevailing currents | ⟶ |

Above: A map showing the routes taken by Columbus on his four voyages to the New World. For the most part he was able to take advantage of the prevailing winds, although on several occasions violent storms caught him unawares.

For the next 13 days strong winds came from the east, and Columbus's little fleet raced across the ocean. Then came five days of slow progress, as the winds dropped and it rained. On September 25 a member of the *Pinta*'s crew claimed to see land, but it was only a low bank of clouds against the western horizon.

The wind picked up again the next day, but by now the crews of all three ships were very unhappy about the length of the journey. A tense mood worsened until on October 10 Columbus was forced to promise to turn around after three more days if no land had been sighted by then. Wet weather and another false sighting of land on October 7 had not helped matters.

By then, however, there were conclusive signs that a large area of land lay nearby. There were more birds visible in the sky, and branches with leaves and flowers were seen floating in the sea around the ships.

At 2 A.M. on October 12 a lookout on the *Pinta* cried out "Tierra! Tierra!" (Land! Land!). The *Pinta* fired a gun. At dawn the low cliffs of an island were visible, and Columbus steered a course around the south of the island. Around noon he landed in a longboat and christened the island San Salvador.

Columbus met some of the San Salvador inhabitants and took six of them on a voyage through the Bahamas. The six served as guides, showing Columbus their traditional canoe route from San Salvador to Cuba.

TEMPTED BY GOLD

Cuba became the goal of Columbus's first expedition. He saw that the native peoples of the Bahamas wore small amounts of gold jewelry. Since the people of these islands were clearly primitive, he reasoned that if they were mining gold, it might easily be taken from them. The precious metal would prove useful back in Europe. There, spices bought from the East were paid for in gold, which at that time was in short supply.

Instead of finding a great Chinese city, they found a village of thatched huts.

On Cuba Columbus heard the word "Cubanacan," which he interpreted as a reference to the great khan, ruler of China according to Marco Polo. He sent two members of his expedition with some native guides inland. But instead of discovering a great city ruled by a Chinese emperor, they found a primitive village of about 50 palm-thatched huts.

Columbus now set sail to the southeast and found another island that reminded him so much of Spain that he called it Hispaniola. He found a very small amount of gold here and some

Hulton Getty

Above: In the hope of finding gold, Columbus sailed eastward along the north coast of Hispaniola.

friendly native people. They told him a story about a place rich in gold—Cybão, which sounded like Cipangu, which was what Spaniards then called Japan.

The story had come from a village farther east, so Columbus set sail for it. On the night of Christmas Eve Columbus's

Below: The Santa María, Columbus's flagship on the first voyage. Although she was slower than the nimble Nina *and* Pinta *that escorted her, her five sails could adapt to subtle shifts in wind conditions.*

flagship, the *Santa María*, was left in the hands of an inexperienced deck-hand and ran aground on a coral reef. No one was killed, but the ship was wrecked. Columbus now had two ships and enough crew for three.

A SETTLEMENT

It was in Columbus's character to find the silver lining in every dark cloud. He decided on Christmas Day that this setback was a sign from God that he should found a settlement here with the crew of the *Santa María*. The first European

THE FIRST SETTLEMENT

Navidad was founded on Christmas Day, 1492, on a small estuary on Hispaniola. Columbus left 39 men, equipped with the wrecked *Santa María*'s stores, to build a fort and look for gold. But tragedy lay in store. During the following months the Spaniards stole the local women and argued over gold. The angry tribes butchered them all in revenge.

Mary Evans Picture Library

Hulton Getty

near Lisbon in Portugal, until March 4. The *Pinta* got separated from the *Nina* during the long voyage from the Azores and fetched up near Vigo on the north-west coast of Spain, at the end of February.

Peter Martyr correctly thought that Columbus had not reached Asia, but few chose to believe him.

News of Columbus's voyage spread rapidly around Portugal, Spain, and Italy and more slowly across the rest of Europe. The general assumption was that Columbus had indeed reached Asia.

However, one perceptive scholar, Peter Martyr d'Anglieri, an Italian living in Spain, described Columbus in a letter to a friend using the Latin phrase "Novis Orbis Repertor" (Discoverer of a New World). Peter Martyr correctly thought that Columbus had underestimated the size of the world, and that he had not traveled far enough to get to Asia. However, this theory was far less exciting than that of Columbus, and few chose to believe the scholar.

colony in the Americas, on the north coast of Hispaniola, was christened Navidad, after the Spanish word for Christmas.

Columbus began the voyage home on January 16, 1493. He first sailed north to avoid the easterly trade winds that had made the journey west relatively easy. He then steered east into a terrible storm, and it took him until February 15 to reach the Azores.

He stayed in the Azores for nine days to rest his weary crew and fix his leaky ship. The rough seas also caused a slow voyage to Europe. The *Nina*, with Columbus on board, did not reach Belem,

Above: The Cubans were eager to trade their goods for Spanish baubles. For their part, the Spaniards were pleased to find docile hosts who might lead them to great riches.

RETURN TO NAVIDAD
Ferdinand and Isabella were much more generous in paying for Columbus's second voyage. Seventeen ships with a total crew of 1,200 left Cadiz on September 25, 1493. The purpose of the voyage was to support and extend the colonization of Hispaniola. They reached the island of Dominica on November 3, 1493, and then sailed on to Navidad.

When Columbus reached Hispaniola on November 25, he discovered that disaster had overtaken the settlement at Navidad. The men he had left behind had taken local women by force and bullied the tribesmen into providing gold. A chief

Barcelona gave Columbus a hero's welcome on his return to Spain in 1493 (below).

named Caonabó had attacked Navidad and slaughtered all the Spaniards.

Because of the unhappy associations of the place Columbus now decided to abandon the site of Navidad. He started a new settlement, named Isabela, 30 miles (48 km) to the east of Navidad. This was founded on January 2, 1494. From here an expedition led by Alonso de Ojeda marched inland looking for gold. Ojeda found three large nuggets in the foothills of the mountains at the center of the island. These, together with some plants he mistakenly thought were cinnamon, pepper, and sandalwood, as well as 26 slaves and 60 parrots, were sent back to Spain with 12 ships of the fleet.

FIGHTING AT THE COLONY

From Isabela Columbus's ships sailed along the south coast of Cuba, which Columbus believed to be the Asian mainland. He also put in to Jamaica. On the way back the ships sailed around the south coast of Hispaniola and anchored off Isabela on September 29.

Once ashore, Columbus found that the colony was in turmoil. Many of the settlers wanted to enslave the islanders and had gone inland taking anything they wanted—including women—regardless of the tribespeople's feelings. They had also begun seizing Native Americans to send back to Spain as slaves.

Columbus tried to control the settlers in order to keep the local people friendly. However, after some of the settlers simply seized three ships and sailed back to Spain, he had no choice but to allow them to do what they wanted.

In March 1495 the first pitched battle between European settlers and Native Americans occurred on Hispaniola. By using dogs and cavalry, the Spaniards were easily victorious. Caonabó, the tribal chief who had destroyed the settlement at Navidad, was captured.

HOPES FADE

A year later Columbus returned to Spain, sailing via Guadalupe. He reached Cadiz in June 1496. By now Ferdinand and Isabella's happy hopes for Columbus's bold enterprise had faded. Whatever he

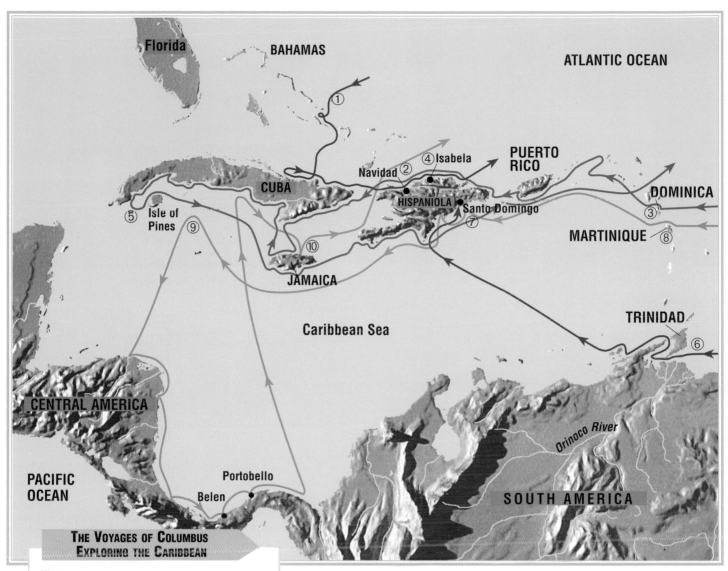

**THE VOYAGES OF COLUMBUS
EXPLORING THE CARIBBEAN**

First voyage ➝
① First landfall, October 1492.
② Foundation of Navidad, December.

Second voyage ➝
③ Reaches Dominica, November 1493.
④ Foundation of Isabela, January 1494.
⑤ Columbus turns back, thinking Cuba is part of Asian mainland.

Third voyage ➝
⑥ Reaches Trinidad, July 1498.
⑦ Columbus arrives in Santo Domingo. In August 1500 the governor arrests him and sends him back to Spain.

Fourth voyage ➝
⑧ Arrives Martinique, June 1502.
⑨ He sails south to explore the coast of "Asia"—in fact Central America.
⑩ Columbus is wrecked and marooned on Jamaica for 12 months.

Mary Evans Picture Library

The Spanish on Hispaniola were soon at odds with the local tribesmen. Fighting broke out in 1495, and the Spanish captured a local chief, Caonabó (above).

The Spanish were keen to find gold, and Columbus sent out expeditions, led by local guides, in search of the precious metal (right).

Columbus eventually fell out of favor and was brought back to Spain in chains (below).

Mary Evans Picture Library

Museo Civico, Turin/Bridgeman Art Library

had found was not China or Japan, and there seemed to be little there worth exploiting. The Spanish rulers approved Columbus's third voyage to the Americas, but only because other European sovereigns were preparing expeditions.

When Columbus discovered the Orinoco, he thought it was the Garden of Eden.

There were fewer volunteers for this voyage, which was to take a riskier route farther south than the previous two. In July 1498 Columbus arrived at the island of Trinidad and sailed along the north coast of South America. By now his eyes were swollen and bloodshot from staring at the horizon. He was also captive to some unlikely medieval theories: when he discovered the mouth of the Orinoco River, he was sure that he had found the site of the Garden of Eden.

From there Columbus sailed north to Hispaniola, where he found the settlers still unhappy with the way he ruled the

LIFE ABOARD THE *SANTA MARÍA*

Life was hard on board a 15th-century vessel—even for the captain or master. On the *Santa María* Columbus slept in a tiny cabin, while the officers slept below deck near the rudder. The crew simply bedded down on straw mattresses in corners of the deck. They kept personal belongings in a sea chest. The only lavatory was the sea itself. When they were not handling the vessel, the crew spent their time in mending sails, pumping the bilges, and other duties.

The variety and quality of the food depended on how recently the ship had docked and revictualed. Basic fare included lard, lentils, salted meat, cheese, and hardtack (biscuit), but fresh produce was picked up whenever possible from ports along the way. There was one hot meal a day, at midmorning. In the tropics of America the biscuit would be reduced to a soggy mess heaving with weevils. When this happened, the crew soaked the hardtack into porridge and ate it in the dark—in order not to see the weevils!

Right: A model of a caravel. The three ships of Columbus's fleet were all caravels. They handled well, but living conditions aboard were primitive.

Science Museum, London/Bridgeman Art Library

colony. In 1500 he found that even Ferdinand and Isabella no longer supported him. They sent a governor to replace him, and Columbus was sent back to Spain under arrest. Although he was never charged with any crime, and was soon released, Columbus never enjoyed his former prestige.

By this time it was known that the islands he had discovered were some distance from Asia. But how far?

THE FINAL VOYAGE

In 1502 Columbus made his fourth and final voyage to the lands he had discovered. His fleet of four ships sailed from Cadiz on May 11 and reached the Caribbean on June 15. He still believed that somewhere to the west of Cuba he would find a strait that would lead to the Far East. His voyage took him along the coast of Central America, and he found some gold but no route to Asia. On his way back to Spain his ships were wrecked on the coast of Jamaica. He and his crew spent a year marooned there, until help came from the colony at Hispaniola. Columbus eventually returned to Spain in November 1504 and died 18 months later in May 1506.

Columbus was an outstanding sailor and navigator who lost very few of his men to shipwreck or disease. He was one of the greatest sea-going explorers, whose discoveries changed the face of the known world of the time.

In Search of a Northwest Passage

News of Columbus's voyage across the Ocean—apparently to Asia—slowly spread through Europe after his return to Spain in 1493. Columbus died believing he had found the coast of Asia. But even before he died in 1506, voyages by other explorers, such as Amerigo Vespucci in 1499, had revealed that a large previously unknown continent extended from Honduras to Brazil.

England was the first country to challenge Spain and Portugal's monopoly of Atlantic exploration. John Cabot, a Venetian merchant who lived in Bristol, asked the English king Henry VII to support a voyage of exploration. Since Cabot was willing to pay the full cost of the voyage, Henry had nothing to lose.

Cabot reasoned that since the world was a globe, and since Columbus had proved "Asia" could be reached by sailing west across the Ocean, then ships sailing in northern latitudes would have a shorter distance to travel than those sailing closer to the equator.

We know only the barest facts about John Cabot's voyages. He sailed from Bristol in May 1497 and reached North

Below: John and Sebastian Cabot receive a blessing before their departure from Bristol in May 1497.

America on June 24. He made his first landfall in Newfoundland or Nova Scotia and sailed partway along the North American coast. In 1498 Cabot left on a second voyage, but it is not certain whether anyone returned from this trip.

John Cabot's son Sebastian is believed to have accompanied his father on the voyage of 1497—he was 12 or 13 at the time. He did not go on his father's second voyage, but he claimed to have sailed in search of a northern route to Asia in 1508. Sebastian reportedly sailed as far north as 58° latitude, more than halfway up the coast of Labrador. Ice and cold prevented him from traveling further.

THE NORTHWEST PASSAGE

Although Sebastian Cabot may not actually have made these voyages, there is no doubt that he believed it possible to sail north of the Americas to Asia. This sought-after route became known among European adventurers as the Northwest

Left: A replica of John Cabot's ship, the Matthew, *left Bristol in May 1997 on a voyage to commemorate Cabot's trip 500 years earlier.*

Western Daily Press

DIVIDING UP THE NEW WORLD

In 1492 a new pope from Aragon in Spain was elected and took as his papal name Alexander VI. After pressure from Ferdinand and Isabella of Spain, Alexander issued a decree on May 4, 1493, that in effect divided up new discoveries between Spain and Portugal. The decree established a line dividing the world 100 leagues (about 300 miles/500 km) west of the Azores. All previously unknown lands found to the east of this line would belong to Portugal, and all those to the west to Spain. In 1494 Spain and Portugal signed the Treaty of Tordesillas, which shifted the "Line of Demarcation" to 370 leagues (about 1,100 miles/1,700 km) west of the Cape Verde Islands.

Right: The Spanish Pope Alexander VI, who signed most of the New World over to Spain.

New York Public Library Picture Collection/Corbis

Left: The privateer Martin Frobisher was financed by a group of London merchants to search for a Northwest Passage to Asia.

Bodleian Library, Oxford/AKG, London

Passage. The uppermost question in the minds of explorers was: "How far north does one have to go?"

Two Portuguese brothers, Gaspar and Miguel Corte Real, sailed west in search of Asia. Both were later lost at sea, Gaspar on a voyage in 1501 and Miguel the following year. However, Giovanni di Verrazano for France and Esteveo Gomez for Spain each explored the North American coast in 1524.

The French explorer Jacques Cartier made three voyages to the mouth of the St. Lawrence River, in 1534, 1535–1536,

In 1576 Martin Frobisher reached the southern coast of Greenland (right). He continued west to Baffin Island, where he sailed up a long inlet, believing it to be a strait. This is now called Frobisher Bay.

John Beatty/Getty Images

and 1541–1542. He brought settlers with him on the last voyage, but they abandoned the colony in 1543.

English explorers made the most dedicated search for the Northwest Passage. Humphrey Gilbert was the leading publicist for it. In 1566 he presented a petition to Queen Elizabeth I, asking permission to be allowed to try to find "a passage by the Northe to go to Cataia [China] & all other east parts of the worlde." A group of London merchants agreed to pay for an expedition in 1576. They chose a gruff, serious-minded privateer named Martin

THE COLONIZING SPIRIT

The first book in English to promote the idea of colonization was written by the soldier-turned explorer Sir Humphrey Gilbert in 1566.

In his *Discourse of a Discovery for a New Passage to Cataia* he wrote: "We might inhabit some part of those countries, and settle there such needy people of our country, which now trouble the common wealth."

Gilbert had seen Protestant Scots settlers in the north of Ireland and believed that what could be done there could be imitated in the New World.

Frobisher as commander. He was given two ships and a little pinnace (a type of small boat) and set sail from London on June 7, 1576.

On July 11 Frobisher reached Cape Farewell, the southern tip of Greenland. He continued sailing west until he found what he thought was a strait (we know it as Frobisher Bay), which he sailed along for 150 miles (240 km). He then turned around and went back to the entrance. On August 19 Frobisher saw "a number of small things fleeing the Sea a farre off, whyche he supposed to be Porposes, or Ceales, or some kind of a strange fishe."

FROBISHER AND THE INUIT

Frobisher had also met some suspicious Inuit. Using sign language, he managed to barter for furs, fresh meat, and salmon. Frobisher's ship fascinated the Inuit, who clambered about the rigging, showing they were "verie strong of theyr armes, and nimble of their bodies."

One Inuit agreed to row his kayak ahead of Frobisher's ship up the strait. But when Frobisher ordered five of his men to take the Inuit ashore in a rowboat, the five sailors were kidnapped instead. An angry Frobisher set sail for home on August 26.

FOOL'S GOLD

Frobisher brought back some glittering rocks to London, and his backers chose to believe they contained gold. There was enough of it around Frobisher Bay to make them a fortune. His backers formed the Company of Cathay to mine the land and to search for the Northwest Passage. In fact Frobisher had brought back worthless "fool's gold" (iron pyrites).

Regardless of the "gold," Frobisher wanted to go back and rescue his five shipmates. He set off with a new expedition and reached the bay in July 1577. He then spent his time searching for his lost sailors and digging for ore. He found no sign of his former crew but plenty of rocks. This time he also brought back an Inuit woman, her child, and an Inuit man he had captured.

Assayers calculated that the 200 tons of ore brought back by Frobisher would pay back a 15 percent profit. This erroneous judgment convinced the Company of Cathay to send yet another expedition the next year.

British Museum, London/Bridgeman Art Library

Lester V. Bergman/Corbis

Rocks of iron pyrites (above) that Frobisher found on Baffin Island were thought to be gold ore.

Snow was falling when Frobisher's 15 ships reached what is now known as Hudson Strait on July 7, 1578. For 20 days the little fleet battled with ice floes and tricky currents, before returning to the familiar bay to the north.

This time the Company of Cathay wanted to found a colony and collect as much of the lustrous ore as possible. However, the icy conditions had continued throughout July and into August. The colonists were not happy about

Above: This drawing of an Inuit man was made by John White, who was on Frobisher's second voyage to America. White was the first European to make drawings of Inuit.

DAVIS'S QUADRANT

John Davis's quadrant, or backstaff, was the greatest navigational invention of the 16th and 17th centuries. The priniciple was simple. Instead of trying to look at the sun, as an astrolabe or simple quadrant demanded, the navigator used the top of a shadow cast by a staff on a scale. The position of this gave an indication of the height of the sun, enabling the latitude to be calculated.

The instrument helped Davis to be a remarkably good navigator for his time. In an age when most calculations of latitude were out by a degree or so, Davis was accurate to within minutes. His skill earned him frequent employment with English and Dutch expeditions sailing to the Far East.

Davis's quadrant (right) was a basically simple device. A navigator achieved best results in calm seas, when the deck would be steady.

Bridgeman Art Library

spending the winter in such a cold and snowy place. So on September 2 Frobisher took the whole party home.

For five years the Company of Cathay tried to smelt gold or silver from the 1,350 tons of rock that Frobisher had brought back. In the end the chairman, Michael Lok, blamed Frobisher for the failure to find anything of value. The Company of Cathay went bankrupt and Frobisher went back to being a privateer.

By the 1580s Humphrey Gilbert was preoccupied with attempts to found a British colony in Newfoundland. Meanwhile his brother Adrian planned a new search for the Northwest Passage in which Humphrey still so ardently believed. Adrian received a charter from the English queen Elizabeth I in February 1585, and he found another privateer, John Davis, to lead the voyage.

JOHN DAVIS IN GREENLAND

Davis, his two ships, and their 42 crew reached Greenland on July 29, 1585. They sailed along the south coast and landed at a bay that had been settled by the Vikings, present-day Godthaab.

Here Davis met some Inuit. They approached his vessel "with great outcryes and skreechings." Davis and a few of his crew disembarked on a rocky island—together with four musicians. They struck up a tune, and the sailors began to dance. Ten of the Inuit decided to investigate the party and rowed their kayaks to the island. Since the Europeans seemed friendly, some bartering took place. Davis and his shipmates got five kayaks and some sealskin garments, while the Inuit received English woolens.

The glaciers of Greenland (above) released vast icebergs into the rocky sounds and bays, creating treacherous conditions for mariners such as John Davis.

On August 1 Davis resumed his voyage north up the strait that is now named after him. He moored off Baffin Island just south of the Arctic Circle, then turned to the southwest and sailed into Cumberland Sound.

Cumberland Sound was an exciting discovery. Unlike Frobisher's Strait, the water there gets deeper as one sails up it, as might be expected of a strait connecting two oceans.

On August 20 Davis was at the point where he might have learned that Cumberland Sound was a dead end when the wind changed. His ships would have had to head into the wind in order to continue their voyage—a difficult maneuver for sailing ships. Since it was late summer, and since the iciness of the waters and winters in this area were known to Davis, he decided to turn around and come back next year.

On his second voyage in 1586 Davis took four ships with him. He ordered two to sail due north between Iceland and Greenland to explore a possible sea route to Asia directly over the North Pole. He took the other two ships back to Godthaab, where Davis and his musicians had entertained the Inuit. This year's trading was accompanied by an energetic athletic contest.

Davis noted that the Inuit were "very simple in their conversation, but marvelous theevish, especially for iron."

The painting below shows Martin Frobisher's party under attack by Inuit in 1577. A few years later Davis's men also came under attack by Inuit at Godthaab in Greenland.

Some Inuit cut a ship's cables in order to get its iron anchor. Davis fired his cannon over the heads of others before they could do the same to the other ship. The Inuit came back the next day, but Davis refused to let them aboard his ships. The angry Inuit now threw rocks at Davis's ships. Davis resisted the demands of his crew to start fighting the Inuit.

For two days Davis refused to trade with the Inuit. They sent an embassy to negotiate with him. Davis captured one as a hostage, promising to release him if

23

the anchor was returned. However, an hour later "the wind came fayre, whereupon we weyed and set saile, and so brought the fellow with us." The captive Inuit later died on the voyage back to England in September.

The two ships that were to explore the polar route sailed partway up the east coast of Greenland but could not get near the shore because of the ice. So they turned around and sailed to Godthaab. They found the Inuit there were angry at the kidnapping by Davis. However, the English soon persuaded them to trade, and they even played a football game.

These happy times ended, however, when the Inuit sold the English a leaky kayak. The dispute ended in a shootout between the two sides. The English killed three Inuit, and one Englishman was wounded. The two ships set sail for home in early September.

NORTH TO BAFFIN BAY

Davis returned for his third and last voyage in the following year. However, this time one of his own ships proved to be leaky. He also had trouble with his crew, most of whom were more interested in making money fishing instead of attempting to find the Northwest Passage.

Davis's patience was clearly running out. Back at Godthaab, he wasted no time in trying to befriend the Inuit; this time he seized a hostage right away. Understandably, the Inuit took revenge and stole all the iron nails out of a pinnace assembled by Davis's crew. Davis loaded the pieces of the boat back on board and turned his back on Godthaab and its Inuit for the last time.

Davis's fleet sailed up Baffin Bay and reached 73° North, where they found pack ice and threatening icebergs. So

Nik Wheeler/Corbis

Fishing in the waters off Newfoundland (left) appealed to Davis's men more than exploring.

Right: A map showing the routes of the first European attempts to find a Northwest Passage. The hardy explorers who nosed into the forbidding inlets between Labrador and Greenland were acting on a hunch—one that would be vindicated three centuries later.

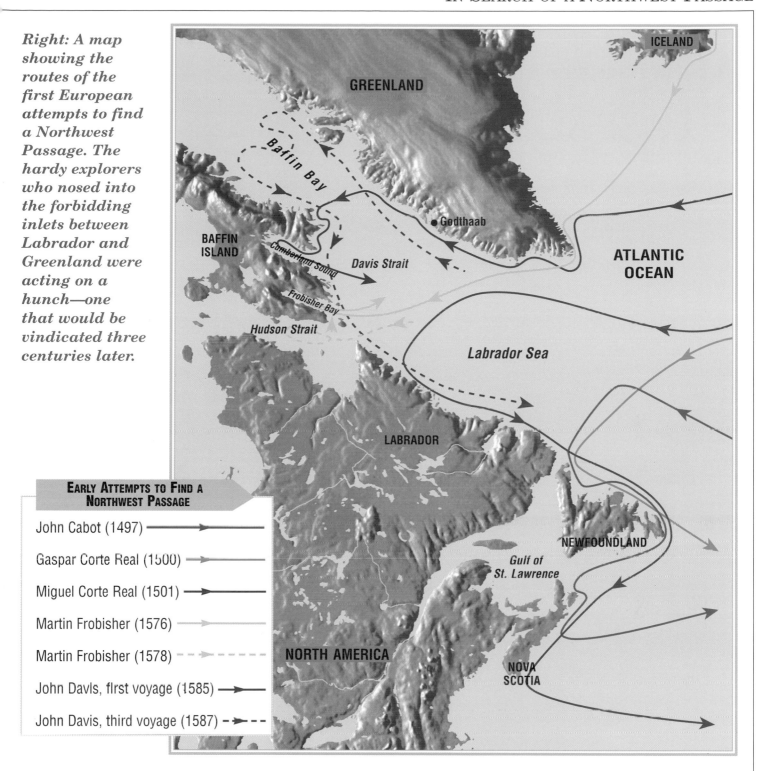

EARLY ATTEMPTS TO FIND A NORTHWEST PASSAGE

John Cabot (1497) ⟶

Gaspar Corte Real (1500) ⟶

Miguel Corte Real (1501) ⟶

Martin Frobisher (1576) ⟶

Martin Frobisher (1578) - - - ⟶

John Davis, first voyage (1585) ⟶

John Davis, third voyage (1587) - ⟶ - -

they turned back to Cumberland Sound and then returned home via Labrador and Newfoundland.

This was as close as anyone ever got to the Northwest Passage during the 16th century. The true route from the Atlantic to the Pacific lies through Lancaster Sound, beyond Baffin Island at 74° North. But even if any daring sea captain had reached as far as Lancaster Sound, he would have had to turn back. No vessel of that time could contend with the Arctic ice floes, which have to be pushed aside by a powerful engine and a strong bow. The Northwest Passage had to wait for a later generation of explorers.

THE NORTHEAST PASSAGE

Englished explorers were slow to copy John Cabot's voyage to North America (or northern Asia, as he believed it to be) in 1497. While Columbus brought back scraps of gold and promised more, Cabot had returned emptyhanded.

In the mid-16th century John Dee calculated that a route to Asia existed "over the top" of Europe. Sailors would have to sail north of the inhospitable North Cape (below) and eastward to Asia.

Some merchants from Bristol in England joined forces with a few Portuguese sea captains to organize another expedition to Newfoundland, but this also came to nothing. Henry VIII, who was crowned king of England in 1509, had no interest in new worlds. For some 50 years there was little exploration by the English. But that all changed in the 1550s.

JOHN DEE'S THEORIES
One of the men most responsible for an upturn in British exploration was John Dee, a mathematician who also studied

geography and other scientific subjects of the day. His research into ancient and medieval authorities, and the news of the voyages of Columbus and other seagoing explorers, led him to conclude that there were five routes to Asia.

One route was around Africa. Another lay through the Strait of Magellan in South America. Just as there was a strait at the south end of what was now called the New World, there would also be a Northwest Passage to the north. Dee also believed that a ship could sail due north, over the Pole, to Asia. His fifth route,

The celebrated mathematician and magician John Dee (right), born in 1527, enjoyed the favor of English royalty. He advised mariners on navigation in both the New World and Eurasia.

Ashmolean Museum, Oxford/e.t. archive

however, was the one he believed offered the best prospects to English merchants and explorers: to sail east from the North Cape of northern Norway to Asia.

Dee's idea came from his studies of Arab geographers, who wrote that the North Cape was the most northerly point of Europe. From there the coast angled southeastward until it reached the easternmost cape of Asia. The most inhospitable part of the voyage was around the North Cape, where summers were short and winters long. From there, however, a course to the southeast would mean sailing into ever-improving conditions.

MERCHANT-ADVENTURERS

As the 1550s began, English merchants took an interest in Dee's theories. Sales of woolen cloth in Europe had fallen, and a search for new markets began. While the European settlers and the nearly naked peoples of the Caribbean were unlikely to buy wool clothes, peoples living along the north coast of the Eurasian

Wolfgang Kaehler/Corbis

Sir Hugh Willoughby (left) laid thorough plans for a combined attempt to find a Northeast Passage. But he underestimated the cold in Lapland (below). His party spent the winter of 1553 there and died from exposure.

Gianni Dagli Orti/Corbis

Willoughby pressed on into the Arctic. He followed an easterly course and hit the island of Novaya Zemlya in August 1553. With the short Arctic summer clearly nearing its end, Willoughby chose to turn back and winter in Lapland. This was a terrible mistake, for he had no conception of how severe winter was in these northerly latitudes. The bitter cold killed him and all his crew.

AN AUDIENCE WITH THE CZAR

Chancellor, meanwhile, followed the coast more closely and put in to Archangel, a Russian port. He persuaded the locals to send him south to Moscow

John Noble/Corbis

landmass might. A group of London merchants created the Company of Merchant Adventurers, which would explore their world and try to trade at the same time. The Northeast Passage was the first goal this new corporation set itself.

The first voyage set out in 1553. Sir Hugh Willoughby, a soldier, led the fleet of three ships, assisted by a navigator, Richard Chancellor. They agreed that if the ships became separated in the North Sea, they would rendezvous at Vardo, a bay on the north coast of Norway.

It was a wise precaution, but the plan still misfired. Chancellor's ship lost the other two in a storm near the Lofoten Islands. By the time Chancellor reached Vardo, Willoughby had been and gone.

by horse-drawn sleigh. Here Chancellor met Ivan the Terrible, Russia's czar. Ivan was desperate for a cheaper alternative to Russia's normal trade route with Europe. (Currently he was sending ships through Baltic seaports controlled by a federation of Baltic and German ports, the Hanseatic League.)

The Russians welcomed the woolen cloth and weapons English merchants could supply, while the English wanted to buy Russian furs, hemp, and tallow for candles. Chancellor returned to England in 1554, with a good report of the warm welcome he had received and Ivan's promise of extensive trading privileges.

Mary Evans Picture Library

In 1554 Richard Chancellor had an audience with Russia's Ivan the Terrible (above), who was eager to trade.

In 1555 Chancellor returned to Russia. When he arrived in Moscow, he was presented with papers from Willoughby's ships, from which he learned about his colleague's fate. Chancellor himself fared no better. He was returning to England in 1556 with the first Russian ambassador when his

AN INSPIRED MAPMAKER

Abraham Ortelius (below), who was born in Antwerp, Belgium, in 1527, worked for a mapmaker as a young man and began his career coloring maps by hand. He later went into business for himself as a map dealer, and his experience at the mapmaker's made him realize how badly informed most maps were. He determined to do his own research for a new atlas and used the firsthand accounts of the explorers who had traveled across the world in the previous century.

Ortelius's own atlas, *Theatrum Orbis Terrarum* ("Picture of the World"), was published in 1570 and set the standard for maps for generations. While there are still mistakes in his maps, in their day they were the best source of geographical information.

ship was wrecked in a terrible storm off Scotland. The ambassador survived, but Chancellor drowned.

BOROUGH'S ATTEMPT

As welcome as the new Russian market was to English merchants, what they really wanted were the spices and silks of Asia. In 1556 a tiny boat with a crew of eight left Gravesend, England, to continue the search for the Northeast Passage. The leader of the expedition was Stephen Borough, who had sailed with Chancellor in 1553–1554. An elderly Sebastian Cabot, now chairman of the Merchant Adventurers' company, visited Gravesend to watch Borough sail and took part in a dance held to celebrate the occasion.

Borough's tiny vessel managed to sail as far east as the Kara Sea before winter set in and prevented further voyaging. Borough wintered at the mouth of the Dvina River, near Archangel, before returning to England the following year.

Borough's tiny vessel sailed as far east as the Kara Sea before winter set in.

Following Borough's failure, the Company of Merchant Adventurers abandoned its former ambitious objective of reaching Asia, because its directors realized that they could make a healthy enough profit buying and selling goods in Russia. Accordingly, they changed their trading name to the Muscovy Company.

John Dee's enthusiasm was for exploration, not making money. He continued to promote the idea of a Northeast Passage, as well as a route to the northwest. In 1580 his efforts resulted in the expedition of Arthur Pet and Charles Jackman. Their two ships followed roughly the same course as Borough's and met the same setback in the Kara

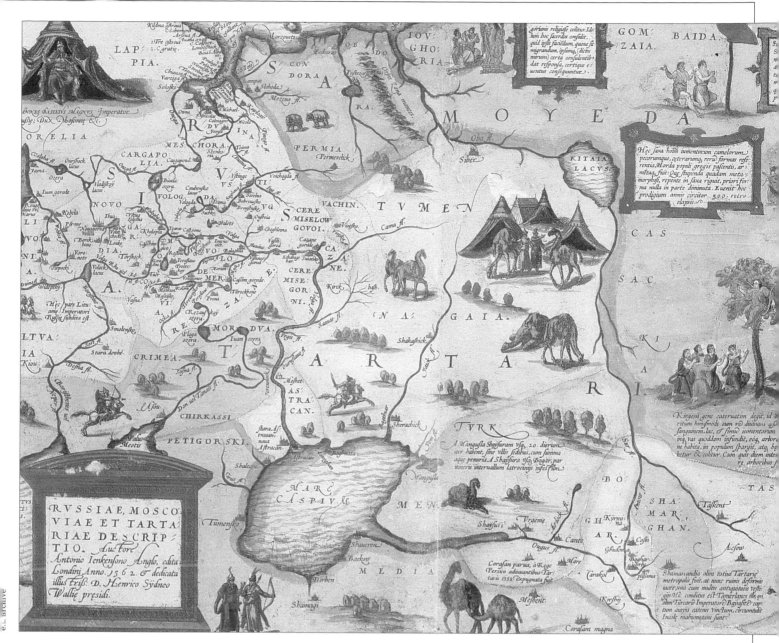

Sea. On the way back Jackman's ship sank off Norway, and Pet thought himself lucky to reach the safety of the Thames.

Dee stubbornly insisted that once through the Kara Sea, sailors would find the coast turning southeast and would enter a less harsh climate. But no one in England was interested any more.

DUTCH EXPLORATION

The Dutch took a different view. They had followed the English into the White Sea, and a Dutch trader had gone overland to the coast of Siberia. Like their

Above: A map of Russia by Ortelius. He consulted the accounts of explorers, and his maps were highly accurate.

Peter Plancius (right) believed that the seas north of Siberia led to Asia.

31

Right: Willem Barents failed to cross the Kara Sea, but he is credited with discovering Spitsbergen and Bear Island—and a sea is named in his honor.

Below: The harsh Spitsbergen Islands gave Barents the first clue that bad weather was on its way.

English counterparts, Dutch merchants also found a geographer, Peter Plancius, whose theories suggested that a route to Asia lay through the seas north of Siberia. They agreed to pay for an expedition commanded by Willem Barents,

e.t. archive

Kevin Schaefer/Corbis

Above: A picture of Barents's men shipwrecked on Novaya Zemlya during his 1596 voyage, drawn by first officer Gerrit de Veer. In the background is the shelter built out of the ship's timbers. The ship's crow's nest can be seen belching smoke; later, the chimney was sealed in order to keep precious warmth inside the hut. In the foreground the sailors are building the boat in which they finally escaped the ice.

who took a fleet of four ships to Novaya Zemlya in 1594. He was accompanied by one of the great Dutch geographers and explorers, Jan van Linschoten.

Van Linschoten had gained national fame for his voyage to the Far East around the Cape of Good Hope. He also lived in India for many years. His book, the *Itinerario*, to be published in 1596, was the standard work used by Dutch navigators for routes around Africa, the Americas, and in the Far East. It was compiled from Spanish and Portuguese books and his own experiences.

While English mariners had tried to find a route around the south of Novaya Zemlya, Barents chose instead to sail around the north. Once he had spotted the island, he followed its coast to the northeast. At the northernmost point of the coast, ice prevented him from continuing further. Meanwhile van Linschoten, who had followed the Russian coast eastward, passed to the south of Novaya Zemlya and entered the Kara Sea.

In 1595 Barents and van Linschoten tried again, this time aiming for the Kara Strait at the south end of Novaya

Right: Sea routes taken over the top of Europe in search of the Northeast Passage. The Novaya Zemlya islands, backed by the icy Kara Sea, blocked the path of all the early attempts.

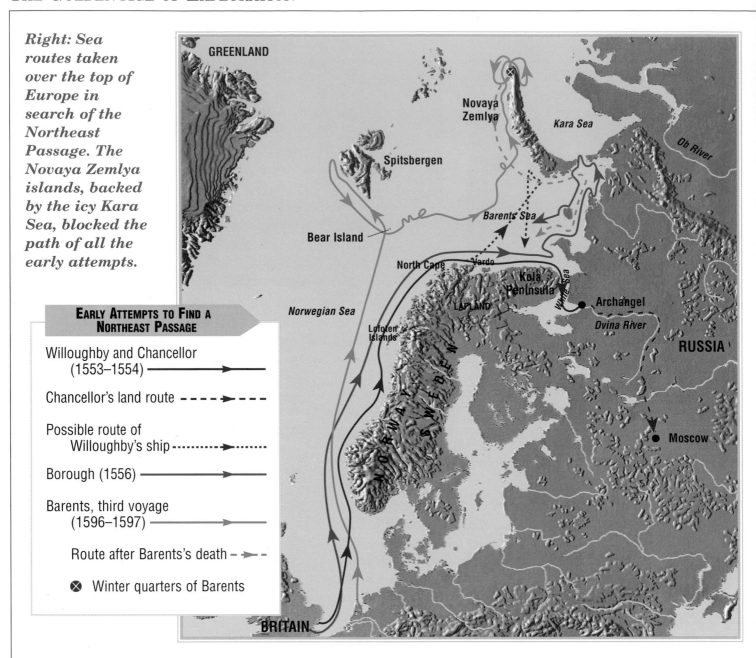

EARLY ATTEMPTS TO FIND A NORTHEAST PASSAGE

Willoughby and Chancellor (1553–1554) ——————▶

Chancellor's land route – – – – ▶

Possible route of Willoughby's ship ·········▶

Borough (1556) ——————▶

Barents, third voyage (1596–1597) ——————▶

Route after Barents's death – ▶ –

⊗ Winter quarters of Barents

Zemlya. But the summer had been very cold, and ice was still blocking the channel. Barents had to turn back.

SHIPWRECKED ON NOVAYA ZEMLYA
Barents's third attempt took place in 1596; this time he was acting as pilot to an expedition of two ships. Since every attempt to get through the Kara Sea had failed, the Dutch ships now sailed north through the Norwegian Sea. In doing so, they discovered the Spitsbergen Islands. One ship then turned back for the Netherlands. The other ship, commanded

by Jakob van Heemskerk and piloted by Barents, ran into polar pack ice. Van Heemskerk turned around and set an eastward course for Novaya Zemlya.

Passing around the north cape of the island, they found the ice closing in again. Gerrit de Veer, the ship's first officer, wrote in his journal, "It was a terrifying spectacle, and the ice moved with the sound of thunder." The ice forced the ship out of the water and crushed the hull. The Dutch sailors had to find shelter on Novaya Zemlya, building a house out of the ship's timbers.

The house was long and large, and the crow's nest of the vessel was placed on the roof to serve as a lookout post. The Dutch built a steam room to help them cope with the severe cold, but it was not enough. The house and its chimney were sealed against the cold, and the sailors choked on smoke from the fire. Their drinks froze in their cups.

The sun vanished below the horizon as winter drew on. The only record of the passage of time they had was an iron ship's clock that ticked away through the endless Arctic night.

For food they trapped foxes and bears and ate scurvy grass. They also hunted seals using halberds. (The weapons were found 300 years later by a Norwegian expedition.) Barents entertained the crew by reading to them from a Spanish history and geography of China.

SAVED BY THE SUN

De Veer recorded the immense relief the Dutch felt when the sun reappeared on the horizon with the simple words: "We gave thanks to God." In June 1597, when enough ice had melted, the Dutch crew were finally able to pack themselves into their ship's longboats and cross the freezing cold waters of the White Sea toward the Kola peninsula. But Barents's health had been destroyed by the winter, and he died on June 19. His companions on the expedition finally got back to Amsterdam in the summer.

Barents had made use of a log that Arthur Pet had kept in 1580. In turn his detailed account of the weather and the charts he made of the coasts around the sea that commemorates his name provide knowledge used by sea captains sailing those waters even today.

Barents's icebound vessel is besieged by polar bears (above). The sailors used halberds to spear the bears, whose fatty flesh helped to keep them alive during the cold and dark winter months.

RICHARD EDEN

Until the mid-16th century there was virtually no English travel literature. This changed with Richard Eden, who in 1553 wrote *A Treatyse of the Newe India,* which told the stories of the voyages of Columbus, Vespucci, Magellan, and Albuquerque.

Two years later Eden followed this with *The Decades of the Newe Worlde, or West India,* which was more detailed than his first book and included the story of the voyage of John Cabot. Eden had interviewed Sebastian Cabot, then a very old man, to get firsthand material for this book.

ROUNDING THE CAPE

The lure of spices drew European explorers south around Africa, just as it lured Columbus across the Atlantic. However, the seagoing explorers who ventured south were not risk-takers like Columbus. Geographers believed that once the west African coast began to curve east, following it would lead to

In the 16th century one huge obstacle blocked a European sea route to India. That obstacle was Africa. In 1487 explorers finally found—and rounded—the Cape of Good Hope (below) at Africa's southern tip.

India. In 1450 the Portuguese knew that Africa stretched as far south as modern Conakry in Guinea, and that the coast continued south as far as the eye could see. But they believed that eventually it would turn east. It was just a question of finding out how far a ship had to go.

EARLY PORTUGUESE EXPLORATION

Unlike Columbus, who ventured into the unknown, Portugal's Prince Henry, called "the Navigator," promoted patient exploration of the African coast. Between 1450 and 1460, the expeditions he sent tried to gain greater knowledge of the Gambia and other West African rivers.

In 1462, two years after Prince Henry's death, Pedro da Sintra made a voyage that is thought to have been planned by Henry. He pushed on past Guinea and the Geba River to the coast of modern-day Liberia. This was the last major advance in geographical knowledge for seven years. The Portuguese king, Afonso, preferred to fight wars against the Muslims of North Africa.

Exploration was resumed in 1469 by Fernão Gomes. King Afonso did not wish to pay for expeditions out of the royal treasury, as Henry the Navigator's efforts had left large debts that were still being paid off.

Instead Afonso sold a lease to Gomes. Gomes paid an annual rent and was required to explore 300 miles (500 km) of coast each year during a six-year period. In return he had total control over all trade in Guinea, except in ivory and civet cats (mammals whose scent secretions were used in the perfume industry).

Gomes did not accompany the expeditions along the African coast himself. He placed an experienced mariner in charge of each exploration. By 1475, the last year of his lease, one of his captains had reached latitude 2° South. The African coast, far from leading east to India, had turned sharply south again.

NAVIGATING AT SEA

This setback occurred at the same time as a war between Castile and Portugal—which could have been the reason why there were no further explorations for nine years. But the Portuguese navigators also faced a tricky technical problem now that they had reached the Equator.

Pilots and navigators hugging the coast on their voyages used landmarks such as headlands, capes, or mountains. But if a ship sailed out of sight of land, how could it know where it was? Modern ships use satellites and precise computer instruments to locate their positions. But

Bibliothèque Nationale de Cartes et Plans, Paris/Bridgeman Art Library

This astrolabe (above) was made in Iraq in the ninth century by Ahmad Ibn Khalaf. The central portion was revolved to take bearings on stars or planets.

in a 15th-century ship the navigator had to use instruments that could almost be made at home. Two were in common use: the quadrant and the astrolabe.

The quadrant was a triangle with one curved side and a piece of string with a lead weight hanging down from the squared angle. The straight edge was used to take a sighting of the Pole Star, and the weighted string showed the height of the star in degrees. To locate a ship's position, a navigator compared the readings taken on the voyage with one taken in the ship's port of origin.

Navigators also used the astrolabe to take sightings of stars and planets. It was circular, with the degrees marked around the outside edge. A movable sight bar was adjusted to get a reading. These readings could then be used like those taken from a quadrant.

The astrolabe was preferred to a quadrant, since a ship on the sea is constantly in motion. The quadrant's weighted string would always swing slightly, and the navigator would have to guess the exact reading. The astrolabe's sight bar would at least stay still.

These instruments gave readings that could be used to discover a ship's latitude. In the 15th century there was no way to calculate longitude accurately. A clock is needed to do this, and while at sea 15th-century navigators had to make do with sand-filled hourglasses.

THE RULE OF THE SUN

With star sightings so important to navigation, the Portuguese sailing southward faced a disturbing problem. As they neared the Equator, the Pole Star gradually sank toward the horizon, until at about 9° North it disappeared altogether.

In 1484 King John II of Portugal summoned a group of mathematicians to find a way of navigating using the sun. They created what became known as the Rule of the Sun. The navigator had to make

D. JOÃO II

Museu de Marinha, Lisbon/Bridgeman Art Library

King John II (above) actively supported Portuguese exploration—partly because it would help him dominate the trade routes.

MEASURING SPEED AT SEA

Mariners in the 16th century could use the speed of the ship to help determine their position. Measuring speed was done by tying a rope, knotted at certain intervals, to a log and throwing the log overboard. The speed with which the knots slipped over the side gave an idea of how fast the ship was traveling—hence the use of the term "knots" even today to describe a ship's speed. By doing this frequently it was possible to learn, in a rough and ready way, how far the ship had traveled.

several sightings of the sun, both before and after noon, using an astrolabe or quadrant. Finding the altitude of the sun at its highest point gave an indication of the ship's current latitude.

The navigator Diogo Cão, who had served in Prince Henry's court, sailed south in 1482, returning to Lisbon in

Bartholomew Diaz's ships (right) sailed south down the west coast of Africa in 1487. A storm blew him out to sea, and when he next sighted land, it was the long-sought southernmost tip of Africa: the Cape of Good Hope.

Two years after Diaz's historic rounding of Africa, Vasco Da Gama set out for India by the same route. Here (below) he is receiving the blessing of the Portuguese king before setting sail.

1484. His experiences crossing the Bight of Benin may have made use of some early version of the Rule of the Sun. Cão sailed for almost 850 miles (1,350 km) out of sight of land, reckoning his position exclusively by astronomical means. The greatest breakthrough, however, was made by Bartholomew Diaz in 1487.

Diaz set sail from Portugal with two caravels and a supply ship. After rounding West Africa, he probably sailed southeast from the coast of modern-day Ghana to the mouth of the Congo River, then followed the coast of Africa as far as Namibia. There he met a storm, and the winds carried him out to sea. When he

found land again, he was at the Cape of Good Hope. He found the coast curving northeastward. At last, the tip of Africa had been reached.

Diaz sailed back to Lisbon with the good news, arriving in December 1488. But it was seven years before another expedition was commissioned to follow up Diaz's discovery. In 1495 King Manuel I of Portugal overrode the decision of his councillors to abandon any attempt to reach India around Africa.

VASCO DA GAMA

The next expedition took almost two years to prepare, and it set sail from Lisbon in July 1497. Its commander, Vasco da Gama, was not a professional sailor, although familiar with navigation by sea. He was a nobleman and a soldier, and the king valued his diplomatic skills.

Da Gama was to take three ships into the Indian Ocean, plus a storeship that would be left on the African coast. Two of the ships were *naos*. The *nao* was a big vessel valued for its capacious hold rather than for its sailing qualities. The third ship was a caravel, the finest type of sailing ship of the era. Between them the ships carried 20 guns—heavy armament for an exploratory expedition.

The fleet sailed to the Cape Verde Islands and on to the southeast. Da Gama then headed out into the mid-Atlantic. He intended to sail southward and then turn east toward the Cape of Good Hope. This would enable him to avoid poor winds in the Gulf of Guinea and to cross the southeasterly winds between the Equator and 30° South.

However, Da Gama miscalculated when he turned east, and arrived at the African coast a little more than 100 miles

In 1497 the Portuguese naval officer Vasco da Gama (left) led the first expedition to sail from Europe to India around the tip of Africa.

Hulton Getty

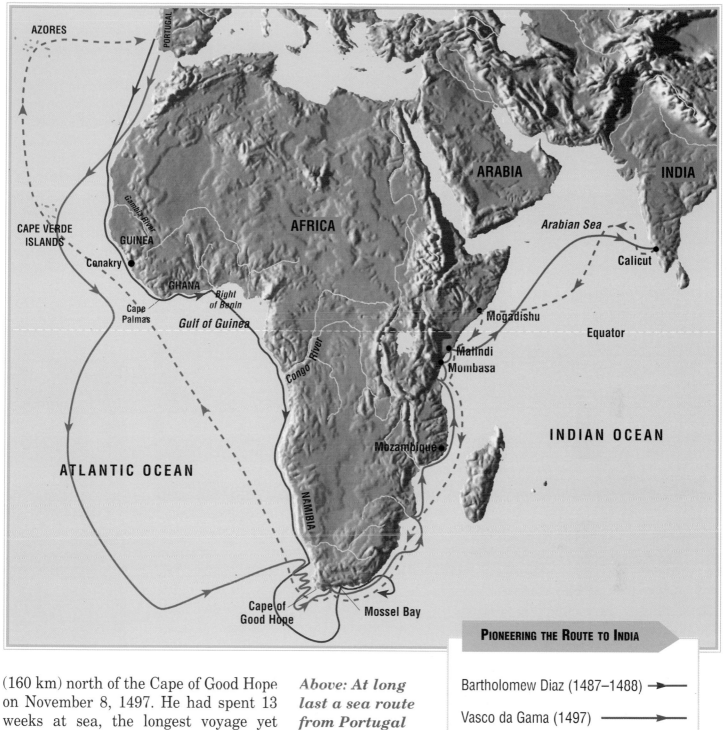

AZORES

PORTUGAL

CAPE VERDE
ISLANDS

GUINEA

Gambia River

Conakry

GHANA

Cape
Palmas

Bight
of Benin

Gulf of Guinea

Congo River

ATLANTIC OCEAN

NAMIBIA

Cape of
Good Hope

Mossel Bay

AFRICA

ARABIA

INDIA

Arabian Sea

Calicut

Mogadishu

Equator

Malindi
Mombasa

Mozambique

INDIAN OCEAN

PIONEERING THE ROUTE TO INDIA

Bartholomew Diaz (1487–1488) →

Vasco da Gama (1497) ⟶

Return voyage 1498–1499 ---▸

(160 km) north of the Cape of Good Hope on November 8, 1497. He had spent 13 weeks at sea, the longest voyage yet made by Europeans.

Wind conditions obliged the ships to sail into the Atlantic then double back to the coast in order to round the Cape. On November 22 Da Gama reached Mossel Bay, on the Indian Ocean coast of South Africa. From here he headed northeast, putting in a couple of times on the coast until he reached Mozambique town.

Above: At long last a sea route from Portugal to India was found. Bartholomew Diaz laid the groundwork, and Vasco Da Gama completed the voyage.

Here the Portuguese found a Muslim sultan who initially thought that the Europeans were also Muslims. Da Gama negotiated with the sultan to get the help of two pilots who knew how to navigate to India across the ocean. Da Gama thought

AKG, London

Left: At Mozambique Da Gama asked the Muslim sultan for a couple of pilots to help him cross the Indian Ocean. But the sultan mistrusted Christians, and Da Gama had to kidnap the pilots.

The Purcell Team/Corbis

he had struck a deal when he offered 2½ lbs. (1 kg) of gold and a roll of silk. But it was not long before the sultan found out that he was dealing with Christians and refused to give the Portuguese any help. Da Gama had to kidnap two pilots and seize a supply of fresh water by force.

Da Gama told the traders: "We come in search of Christians and spices."

The pilots kept giving Da Gama wrong information, and at Mombasa in Kenya, they jumped overboard and escaped. The Mombasans learned from the pilots that Da Gama intended to sail to India. Trade in the Indian Ocean was a monopoly of the various Muslim rulers of the region, and they did not want to do business with Christian Europeans. The Mombasans tried to capture one of Da Gama's ships, but the Portuguese discovered the plot after torturing a hostage they had taken in Mozambique. They left Mombasa without a pilot and followed the coast to the next major port, Malindi.

Here they found a warm welcome. The rulers of Mombasa and Malindi were great rivals, and the sultan of Malindi seems to have taken Da Gama for a Hindu. The people of Malindi greeted his arrival with shouts the Portuguese heard as "Christ, Christ," but probably were "Krishna, Krishna."

Da Gama's luck went further. At Malindi there just happened to be the greatest navigator in all the Indian

Ocean. Ibn Madjid, a pilot from Gujerat in India, had written *Al Muhet*, the standard book of sailing instructions for the Indian Ocean. It is possible that Ibn Madjid piloted Da Gama's ships for the rest of their journey to India, but historians do not know for sure.

ACROSS THE INDIAN OCEAN

With the help of a pilot Da Gama put the coast of Africa behind him and set sail for India. On May 20, 1498, the three ships that had left Lisbon nine months before arrived in Calicut harbor on India's Malabar Coast. A convict who had been pardoned on condition he did dangerous tasks on the voyage was put ashore. He was taken to two Muslim traders who spoke Spanish and said to them: "We come in search of Christians and spices."

The Muslim traders must at once have been alarmed. Muslim merchants had a total monopoly on the spice trade. But religious preferences were no obstacle to the Hindu Indian spice dealers: it made no difference to them whether a trader was Christian or Muslim, as long as they received a good price in either gold or goods for their wares.

What could Da Gama possibly offer in return? After a nine-month voyage his ships would hardly have looked impressive. He had brought with him olive oil, honey, pots, striped cloth, and bells. The technologically backward people of the Caribbean might have welcomed these

Below: Secluded sands near Mombasa in southern Kenya, Africa. It was there that Da Gama's troublesome African pilots jumped ship and abandoned him. Da Gama had better luck in Malindi farther north.

THE DUTCH EAST INDIA COMPANY

Mary Evans Picture Library

Portugal, a small country with a small population, always had difficulty getting sailors for its ships to the Far East. Many Dutch sailors were willing to ship with the Portuguese, but it was only a matter of time before some decided to go into business for themselves in spices.

The groups of businessmen who financed these expeditions formed private partnerships. In 1602 the Dutch parliament agreed to join them together in the Dutch East India Company. The leaders of Dutch expeditions to the Far East now had more authority, since they all belonged to a single powerful corporation rather than one of a number of partnerships.

Left: Businessmen of the Dutch East India Company meet to discuss affairs.

trifles, but the Indians were of an advanced civilization with a history far more ancient than that of Portugal.

A MURDER ATTEMPT

Da Gama spent three months in Calicut. The Hindu king allowed him to sell his goods if he could find a buyer. However, Muslim traders convinced some Hindu noblemen that Da Gama was a pirate. They confined him to his house and tried to murder him. Da Gama escaped, but it was difficult for him to sell his cargo.

He eventually got some pepper and cinnamon, but more importantly he obtained a letter from Calicut's ruler to Portugal's. It read: "In my kingdom there is abundance of cinnamon, cloves, ginger, pepper, and precious stones. What I seek from your country is gold, silver, coral, and scarlet." Da Gama could at least bring King Manuel hope.

In August 1498 Da Gama departed from Calicut. The winds that favored his voyage to India were now against him, and it took him three months to sail back to Malindi. One of his ships had to be abandoned there because so many of his crew had died through disease.

Da Gama reached the Cape of Good Hope on March 20, 1499. Once around the Cape, he found familiar waters. A storm caused the two surviving ships to separate, and the *Berrio*, with Nicolas Coelho in command, reached Portugal in July. Da Gama made a lengthy stopover in the Cape Verde Islands and did not reach Lisbon until September.

CABRAL'S SUCCESS

Da Gama's success inspired King Manuel to send out a second expedition. In March 1500 13 heavily armed ships left Lisbon under the nobleman Pedro Cabral. This epic expedition made the fastest journey ever from Europe to India prior to the invention of the steamship.

From the Cape Verde Islands Cabral sailed far to the southwest and landed in what is now Brazil. He claimed the land for Portugal, then recrossed the Atlantic, rounded Africa, discovered Madagascar and the Horn of Africa, and set up the first European settlement in India.

When Cabral's colony at Calicut was attacked by Muslim traders, he declared war. His superior guns sank 10 Arab ships and

Pedro Cabral (left) led a large Portuguese expedition to India in 1500–1501 and set up the first European settlement there.

bombarded Calicut. Cabral then moved on to Cochin. When he eventually returned to Portugal in 1501, he had the richest cargo of spices ever seen in Europe.

A succession of Portuguese naval leaders destroyed Muslim supremacy in the Indian Ocean. Francisco d'Almeida crushed the Egyptian fleet at the battle of Diu in February 1509, while Afonso

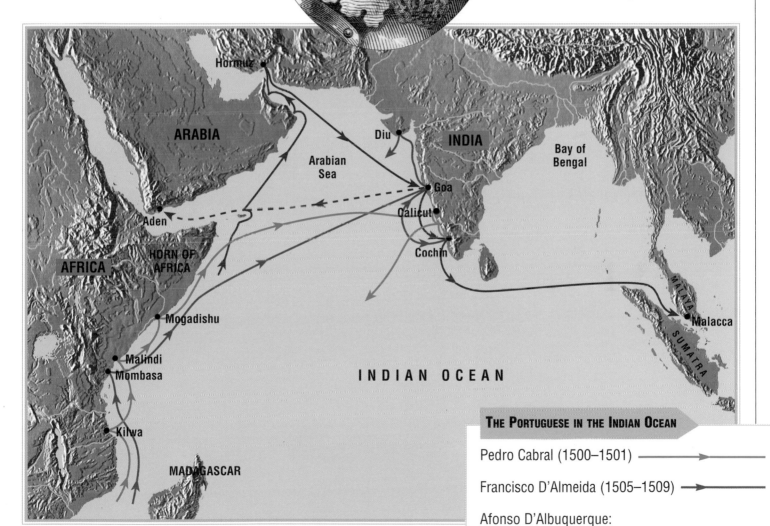

Above: Portuguese trade in the Indian Ocean took off with Pedro Cabral, who used military muscle to establish dominance over Muslim trading fleets.

THE PORTUGUESE IN THE INDIAN OCEAN

Pedro Cabral (1500–1501) ⟶

Francisco D'Almeida (1505–1509) ⟶

Afonso D'Albuquerque:

1507–1511 ⟶

1513 - - - - - - - - - ⟶

THE CARRACK

At the end of the 15th century the largest merchant ship was a carrack. The carrack was three-masted, with a high sterncastle and forecastle. The fore- and mainmasts were square-rigged, while the mizzen mast had a lateen (triangular) sail. These ships were difficult to maneuver but could withstand rough seas well.

The carrack could carry more than 600 tons of cargo—a cargo of 1,000 tons was not unknown. It could also be heavily armed, and the Portuguese used carracks extensively in their wars with the Muslim traders of the Indian Ocean.

Versatile and rugged, the carrack (below) brought Portugal power and riches in the East.

D'Albuquerque founded the four major naval bases of Portugal's Oriental empire: Hormuz, Goa, Malacca, and Aden.

The route to the riches of the East was now open. In 1511 a Portuguese naval force pushed through to Sumatra and the East Indies, and onward to Ceram. One of the vessels was commanded by Francisco Serrano. He investigated the Spice Islands (Moluccas) and established a Portuguese trading post there.

Portuguese naval supremacy allowed the explorers Fernão Pinto and St. Francis Xavier to reach the Far East. Pinto robbed and pillaged, while Francis Xavier preached the Christian gospel

Hulton Getty

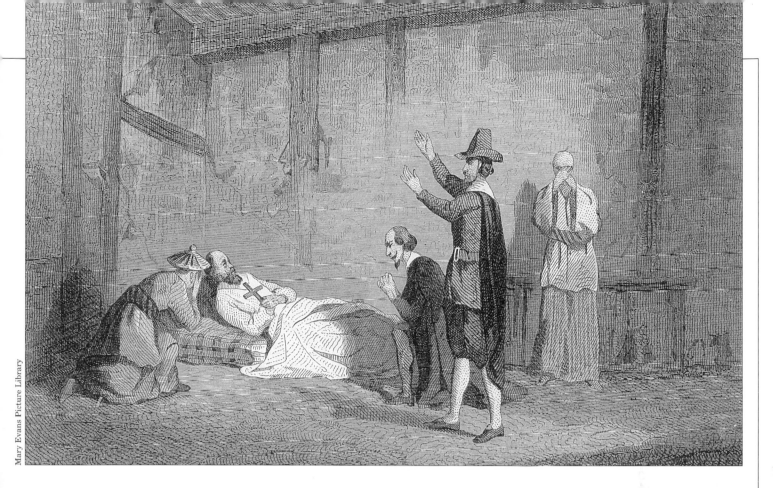

Above: St. Francis Xavier on his deathbed in China in 1552. He and Fernão Pinto were among the first Europeans to visit Japan (right).

until his death in China in 1552. The wealth their ventures revealed attracted attention in other European countries.

In the late 16th century Dutch sailors such as Jan Linschoten and Cornelius Houtman and the Englishman James Lancaster followed the route to the East. Portugal's empire was built by conquering the Muslim fleets, and it would be lost through defeat at the hands of her Protestant rivals.

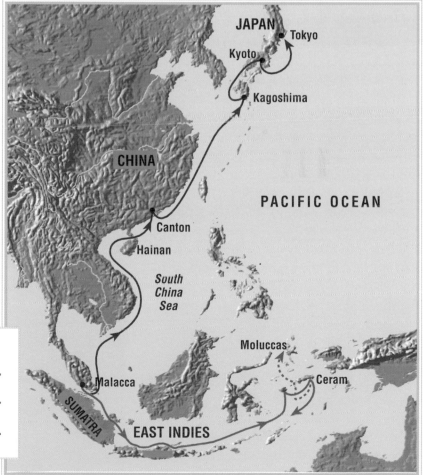

Voyages to the Far East

Portuguese naval force (1511) ——————→

Francisco Serrano's ship - - - - -▶- - -

St. Francis Xavier (1549) ——————▶

PRIVATEERS
AND THE
NEW WORLDS

The Caribbean lands discovered by Columbus soon attracted plenty of settlers. The Spanish *conquistadores* overthrew the powerful civilizations of the Aztecs in Mexico and the Incas in South America to make the New World safe for settlement.

These Spanish colonies developed close trade links with Spain. The colonists wanted clothing, weapons, household utensils, wine, and olive oil. To pay for them they traded gold and silver,

---

A river of silver was soon flowing along the Pacific coast and on to Spain.

---

animal hides, and sugar. The Spaniards created massive farming estates, or plantations, where slaves (originally Native Americans and later captives from West Africa) toiled in the fields.

The real boom in Spanish America occurred in 1545, when prospectors discovered a silver mine at Potosí, Bolivia. In 1548 a similar discovery at Zacatecas, also in Bolivia, insured that a river of silver was soon flowing its way along the Pacific coast, across the Isthmus of Panama, and then to Spain.

TWO-WAY TRAFFIC
Although Ferdinand Magellan had sailed east to west across the Pacific Ocean in 1519–1521, no one had yet succeeded in sailing back the other way. Because there were no charts, sailing the Pacific was still considered a risky thing to do.

Barnabas Bosshart/Corbis

Hulton Getty

Above: The silver mine in Potosí, Bolivia, in Spanish America. Silver mines gave Spain the wealth it needed to fund its expensive expeditions in the New World.

Left: The Inca stronghold Machu Picchu in the Andes, which escaped discovery by the Spanish.

In 1527 the conqueror of Mexico, Hernando Cortes, outfitted three ships and sent them in search of islands in the Pacific where Native-American rumor suggested gold might be found. Two ships were lost at sea, but one, under Alvaro de Saavedra, reached the Moluccas. When Saavedra tried to sail back to Mexico, his unfamiliarity with the winds and currents condemned him to failure. Cortes tried again 10 years later, but the venture ended in a mutiny. The mutineers killed their commander, Fernando Grijalva, and were shipwrecked off New Guinea. There were other fruitless attempts during the 1540s and 1550s to cross the Pacific from the Americas and then sail back again. But it was not until 1565 that a Spanish expedition finally succeeded in doing this.

Miguel Lopez de Legaspi took a fleet westward across the Pacific to the Philippines, where he established a Spanish settlement on the island of Cebu. With him as pilot traveled an experienced Pacific navigator—Andres de Urdaneta. Urdaneta was eager to try to navigate back to Mexico, although all earlier attempts had been thwarted by the northeast trade winds. So Urdaneta chose a new route.

On June 1, 1565, he sailed north from the Philippines, reaching latitude 42° North, where he picked up the north-

Hernando Cortes (below) conquered Mexico for Spain in 1519. He later sent ships out into the Pacific to search for islands said to be rich in gold.

Hulton Getty

Tony Arruza/Corbis

easterly Japan current and then the easterly North Pacific current. He reached Santa Rosa Island off southern California before coasting down to Acapulco, Mexico. He had pioneered a new Pacific route—one that would be used for two centuries by galleons carrying the riches of the Philippines to Spain.

News of Urdaneta's achievement spread rapidly through the government of Spanish America. In 1567 Alvaro de Mendana, the nephew of the viceroy of

Peru, took command of an expedition sailing west across the Pacific from Peru. Mendana discovered the Solomon Islands but not the southern continent he expected to find. He returned to Peru using Urdaneta's Passage, as the northern Pacific route was called, arriving there in 1569.

In 1595 Mendana attempted to find the Solomon Islands again, but failed. Instead he discovered the Marquesas. With Mendana sailed his navigator,

The Andes Mountains (above) formed a huge barrier to transporting goods over the interior of South America. So most goods were carried by coastal shipping.

Pedro Fernandez de Quiros, who became obssessed with converting the natives of the South Sea Islands. In 1605 Quiros sailed in search of a mythical southern continent. He reached the New Hebrides, set up a settlement, then after three weeks suddenly took his ship back to South America. His deputy, Luis Vaez de Torres, abandoned the settlement and sailed to the Philippines. He discovered the strait that bears his name, between New Guinea and Australia.

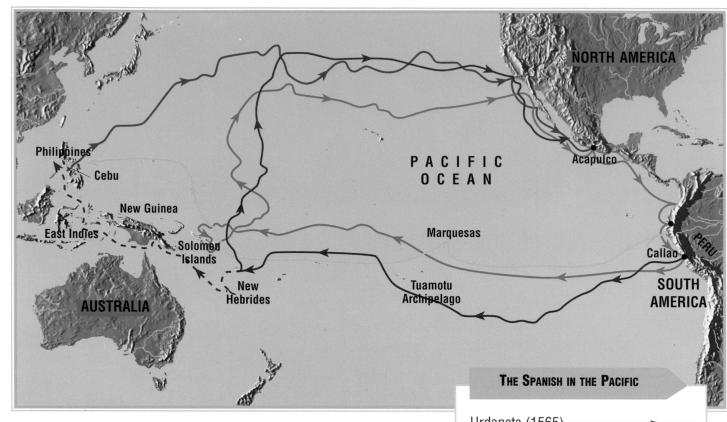

Above: A map showing the pioneering voyages of the Spanish to open up two-way traffic in the Pacific.

Below: Pack trains such as these were used to carry goods across the narrow Isthmus of Panama from one coast to the other.

THE SPANISH IN THE PACIFIC

Urdaneta (1565)	———→
Mendana (1567–1569)	———→
Mendana & Quiros (1595–1596)	—→
Quiros (1605–1606)	———→
Continuation of Quiros expedition under Torres (1606–1607)	- -→ - - -

The rugged terrain of the Andes Mountains in western South America and of tropical Central America insured that coastal shipping carried most of the trade. Vessels sailed north from Peru or south from Mexico to the Isthmus of Panama. Pack trains then carried the goods across the Isthmus to the Caribbean or Pacific coasts.

The towns of Nombre de Dios and Puerto Bello on the Caribbean coast of Panama were busy commercial centers. Goods from Europe arrived there, and the convoys to Spain left from there.

Spain's economy now depended on convoys of galleons linking the far-flung American colonies with mainland Spain. The convoy system began in 1542 during the fourth in a series of wars between Francis I, king of France, and Charles V, king of Spain and Holy Roman emperor.

The system was expensive and inflexible. Merchants had to pay extra duty to fund the cost of the armed galleons. They could also only ship goods when it was convenient for the convoy. A merchant

John Hawkins (right) upset the Spanish when he took his own vessels to trade in the New World colonies.

Heavily armed Spanish galleons (below) sailed back from America laden with booty.

Mary Evans Picture Library

Mary Evans Picture Library

who had tied up a lot of money in a shipment could not pay bills until the cargo had been sold. The rigid trade system created ideal opportunities for smugglers. They could deliver goods at more convenient times and at a lower cost.

The first smugglers were Portuguese. They sailed from Europe with cloth and metal tools and utensils. They journeyed first to Africa, where they added slaves to their cargo, and then across the Atlantic to the Plate River. Pack trains carried the cargoes up into the Andes. The slaves were sold to mine owners in Bolivia, and the other goods went on to the Spanish settlements in Peru, where they could compete in price with the legally shipped but heavily taxed cargoes brought down from the Isthmus.

THE FIRST ENGLISH SLAVE TRADER

In 1562 John Hawkins, from Plymouth in England, decided to try to do in the Caribbean what Portuguese smugglers

Sally Morgan: Ecoscene/Corbis

PRIVATEERS—A LICENSE FOR PIRACY

In the 16th century naval wars in Europe and the Americas were mostly little more than state-organized piracy. Governments and sovereigns granted ship-owners "letters of marque" that authorized them to attack ships flying the flag of the ruler's enemies.

Merchant ships sailing up the English Channel during the 1550s ran a gauntlet between two sets of French privateers (one set from each side in the French civil war between Catholics and Protestants), plus English privateers preying on French Catholic shipping. Spain supported the Catholic side, and during the 1560s Spanish ships were frequently victims of English and French Protestant privateers.

The French Protestants in return established a base in Florida from which they attacked Spanish shipping in the Caribbean. It hurt Spanish shipping sufficiently for King Philip II to order the base's destruction in 1565. Throughout the 1580s Raleigh's efforts at founding a colony were in part an attempt to imitate this French Protestant base during the naval war that then raged between England and Spain.

Tenerife (above) was a stopping point for John Hawkins on his way to West Africa in 1562. There he hired a pilot who could navigate his four ships (including a stolen slave ship) around the Caribbean.

54

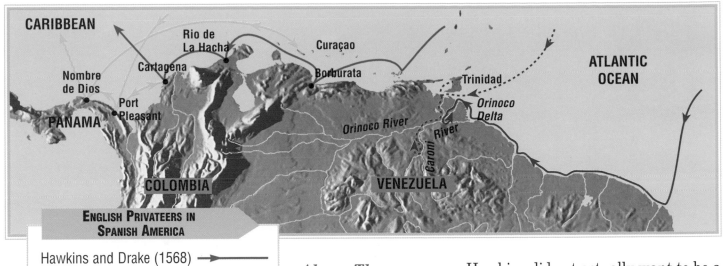

CARIBBEAN

Rio de
La Hacha

Curaçao

Cartagena

Borburata

Nombre
de Dios

Trinidad

ATLANTIC
OCEAN

Port
Pleasant

Orinoco
Delta

PANAMA

Orinoco River

Caroni River

COLOMBIA

VENEZUELA

ENGLISH PRIVATEERS IN SPANISH AMERICA

Hawkins and Drake (1568)	⟶
Drake (1572–1573)	⟶
Raleigh (1595)	----⟶----
Raleigh (1617)	⟶

Above: The routes taken by British privateers preying on Spain's colonies in the Americas.

Below: Philip II of Spain with his third wife, Elizabeth. Philip had no intention of giving the British a share in the riches of his colonies.

were doing in South America. Hawkins had voyaged to the Canaries several times already to trade in the free ports there. He no doubt learned there what Portuguese smugglers were doing and obtained background information on the West African slave trade and West Indian markets from an Italian merchant in Tenerife.

Hawkins found plenty of backers for his triangular trade project. He outfitted three ships in Plymouth and set sail in October 1562 for West Africa. He stopped in Tenerife, where he hired a pilot from Cadiz who knew the Caribbean waters.

In Sierra Leone Hawkins bullied some Portuguese slave traders into selling him 300 slaves and set a westward course with a stolen Portuguese slave ship. He reached Hispaniola, where he sold the slaves to the Spanish plantation owners. With the money he received for the slaves he was able to buy a cargo of goods from the West Indies that included sugar from the plantations and animal hides. Hawkins returned to England in 1563 and was able to sell all his goods at a very large profit.

Hawkins did not actually want to be a smuggler. He would have preferred to trade legally with the Spanish colonies, but the Spanish government proved unwilling to alter its rules. The officials he dealt with in the Caribbean did not have the authority to grant him a license.

A DIPLOMATIC INCIDENT

When complaints from the Portuguese slave-traders in Africa arrived in Lisbon, and his cargoes were seized by the authorities in Seville, Hawkins's enterprise had turned into a diplomatic incident.

The British suggested a compromise to Philip of Spain. If the Spanish authorities allowed Hawkins to trade in the Caribbean, he would protect the Spanish

E. T. Archive

colonies from French privateers. Philip's administration turned the deal down.

A SECOND EXPEDITION

Hawkins set out with four ships on a second voyage in October 1564. This time he had powerful backers in Queen Elizabeth I and high-up officials of the British navy. This time he used more force in both West Africa and the Caribbean. While he was away, however, Philip appointed a tough soldier, Pedro Menéndez

In 1568 Spanish ships attacked John Hawkins's fleet in the Mexican port of San Juan de Ulua (above). Hawkins escaped with a single ship.

de Avilés, to clear the French privateers out of Florida. Philip also tightened up the regulations for the convoy system.

In 1566 Hawkins sent a new expedition, commanded by his associate John Lovell and including Hawkins's cousin, the young Francis Drake. The Lovell expedition did not achieve as great a profit as the previous two. The Spanish authorities were more hostile, since Philip threatened severe penalties for anyone who encouraged the English to trade.

Hawkins's next trading expedition again included Drake. In 1567 he took five ships to Africa where he picked up a cargo of slaves. He then sailed to the Caribbean and the Spanish ports in South America where he sold his cargo.

Off the coast of Mexico one of his ships was damaged in a storm, so he put in to San Juan de Ulua for repairs. The English ships were still in port when the Spanish treasure fleet arrived. The Spaniards suspected that the English planned to attack, although the English ships were heavily outgunned.

The Spaniards attacked the English fleet and defeated them. Hawkins was lucky to escape with one ship. The Spanish condemned the prisoners they took to an eight-year imprisonment.

DRAKE'S REVENGE

Drake returned to the Caribbean in 1571 in a single vessel. An ardent Protestant, he vehemently despised Catholics, and his experience in the Mexican harbor of San Juan de Ulua motivated him to conduct a crusade against the Spanish in the New World. His 1571 voyage was a scouting expedition that he would follow with a bigger venture. He sailed to the Isthmus of Panama and collected information about the coast and harbors in the area. He discovered a harbor that was a perfect base for an attack on nearby Nombre de Dios.

In 1572 he returned with two ships and 73 men. On July 28 he attacked and looted Nombre de Dios. He then led his men inland and captured a pack train laden with gold that was bound for Nombre de Dios and the Spanish treasury there. It was while he was in Panama that Drake climbed a mountain

Francis Drake (right), who first sailed to the Caribbean with his cousin John Hawkins, was to become a notorious privateer.

SILVER AND THE SPANISH

When the Spanish colonists discovered rich silver deposits in Mexico, Bolivia, and Peru during the 16th century, they had found an important new source of income. At that time Spain held sway over parts of Italy, the Netherlands, Belgium, Hungary, and Bohemia, and dearly needed money to finance its colonies.

For the next century or so, vast quantities of the precious metal were mined from the Americas. Spain flooded other European states with silver in exchange for goods and materials to prop up its New World colonies, equip its armies, fund the extravagances of the royal court, and pay off foreign creditors.

However, the newfound prosperity turned out to be an illusion. Having relied so heavily on imports, Spain had neglected to put money into building up its own industrial base. Money from the silver simply ebbed away. By the end of the 17th century Spain had become one of Europe's poorest nations.

Mary Evans Picture Library

and gazed down on the Pacific Ocean—the first Englishman to see it. He vowed that one day he would sail it. Drake spent six months raiding in the Caribbean and returned to England in April 1573 with a huge haul of treasure.

RALEIGH'S DREAM

Not all English adventurers were as aggressive as Hawkins and Drake. The wealthy English adventurer Sir Walter Raleigh had long wanted to found an English colony in the Americas. Raleigh paid for an expedition led by Philip Amadas and Arthur Barlow that reached the North Carolina coast in July 1584.

Below: As this illustration suggests, there is a popular belief that Walter Raleigh accompanied his founding expedition to Virginia in 1584. In fact it is now believed that he never set foot in the ill-fated colony at Roanoke.

They reported, "We found the people . . . void of all guile and treason, and such as lived after the manner of the golden age. The earth bringeth forth all things in abundance, without toil or labor."

In December 1584 money started rolling in to finance Raleigh's colony. In January Queen Elizabeth I gave him permission to call his new land Virginia, in honor of the "Virgin Queen," as she was called, and also allowed him to use one of her ships in his next expedition.

After careful preparations a fleet of seven ships left Plymouth, England, in April 1585, with Richard Grenville in command. Grenville first went raiding in

Mary Evans Picture Library

the West Indies and then arrived near Cape Fear in North Carolina. A colony was set up on Roanoke Island, and the ships returned to England.

THE DREAM BEGINS TO FADE
In the spring of 1586 Francis Drake arrived with a fleet of 23 ships, bringing reinforcements and new supplies to the colony. However, skirmishes with the Native Americans of the area and the failure to find a better site for the colony had left the settlers disheartened. Drake offered to take them back to England, and they agreed.

Raleigh tried again the following year, sending out a new colonizing party under John White. But the Native Americans no longer welcomed the English. Raleigh's first colony had been incapable of fending for itself during the winter and had forced the Native Americans to supply them with food. In August an English privateer dropped anchor off Roanoke, and the colonists sent their governor, John White, back to England to plead their case for more aid.

Raleigh's attempt to reinforce his colony was delayed in 1588 by the Spanish Armada, the naval invasion force sent against Britain by Philip II of Spain. John White was only able to accompany a relief expedition in 1590, and this spent several months privateering in the West Indies before sailing up the coast to Roanoke. They found the settlement abandoned, and the fate of the colonists remains unknown.

THE SEARCH FOR EL DORADO
Raleigh's attention now shifted south to the Caribbean coast of South America. He set out to find a rich kingdom of gold ruled by the fabled El Dorado, Spanish for "The Gilded One." In February 1595 Raleigh left England and sailed to Trinidad and from there to the mouth of the Orinoco River. He collected some

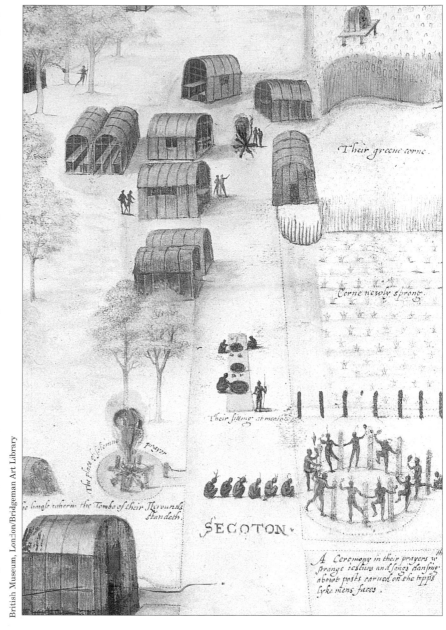

British Museum, London/Bridgeman Art Library

Above: This drawing of a Native-American village was made by John White, who led parties in 1587 and 1590 to support the ill-fated British colony on Roanoke Island.

valuable-looking rocks, which he brought back to England. But no one was interested in a colony in this tropical region. Although he made a second trip to the Orinoco in 1617, Raleigh's dream would remain a dream.

Privateers like Hawkins and Drake increased the amount of detailed navigational knowledge in England about the Caribbean. But unlike their Spanish victims, who built cities like Cartagena and Lima and found a way to cross the Pacific from Asian waters, their grand ideas had few lasting results.

AROUND THE WORLD

Like the first momentous voyage of Christopher Columbus in 1492, Ferdinand Magellan's voyage across the Pacific Ocean in 1520–1521 had its origin in a mistaken idea about the geography of the world.

Columbus had disagreed with the conventional wisdom about the size of the Earth. And Magellan believed the Spice Islands lay fairly close to South America—he completely underestimated the size of the Pacific Ocean.

CLAIMING THE SPICE ISLANDS

Spain and Portugal had divided the world between them in the Treaty of Tordesillas. All territory east of 134° longitude and west of 46° longitude belonged to Spain; the rest was Portugal's. If Magellan's theory was true, the Spice Islands belonged to Spain.

Magellan was a Portuguese nobleman who had already been to the Spice Islands in the first Portuguese expedition of 1511. In 1512 he returned to Portugal, and in 1517 he moved to Seville, in Spain.

After his experience of sailing around Africa, Magellan concluded, as had Columbus, that it would be easier to sail to the Spice Islands by heading west from Europe. The Spanish explorer Vasco de Balboa had already discovered that the Pacific Ocean lay on the other side of the Isthmus of Panama. Magellan believed that sailing south along South America would bring him to a strait connecting the Atlantic and Pacific Oceans. A ship would be able to sail west through the strait and then on across the Pacific

to the Spice Islands. He took his proposal to the Spanish monarch and Holy Roman emperor, Charles V.

Charles agreed to pay for an expedition of five ships under Magellan's command. While Magellan desired Charles V's support, it proved a very mixed blessing. An influential bishop, Juan Fonseca,

In 1517 Magellan planned to sail by a westward route to the Spice Islands (below) in the Pacific Ocean.

Jack Fields/Corbis

insured that key jobs in the expedition were filled by his relatives and friends. Fonseca's appointees included three of the ship's captains (Juan de Cartagena, Luis de Mendoza, and Gaspar de Quesada), the fleet accountant (Antonio de Coca), and the commander of the soldiers (Gonzalo Gómez de Espinosa).

Ferdinand Magellan (right) was determined to reach the Spice Islands, and Charles V of Spain agreed to finance an expedition of five ships.

Hulton Getty

Magellan's expedition, known as the Moluccas' Fleet, left Spain on September 20, 1519. He had five ships—the flagship *Trinidad*, the *San Antonio*, the *Victoria*, the *Concepción*, and the *Santiago*. From Sanlucar they sailed to Tenerife in the Canaries. There Magellan was warned that Cartagena, Mendoza, and Quesada planned to kill him and take over the fleet. Magellan sailed off to the south, hoping to avoid a Portuguese squadron on its way to intercept him.

IN THE DOLDRUMS

Around latitude 8° North Magellan went back to a southwesterly heading. He had escaped the Portuguese squadron, but his alternative route brought him into the Doldrums—an area near the Equator between the northern and the southern trade winds. Both masses of air rise there, so at the sea's surface winds are unreliable. A sailing ship makes slow progress, and the heat and thunderstorms make a passage unpredictable.

In the Doldrums Cartagena noted the growing unhappiness among the crew of the Moluccas' Fleet and challenged Magellan's authority. Magellan had Cartagena placed under arrest in Mendoza's custody, and Antonio de Coca was given command of the *San Antonio*.

Magellan reached the coast of Brazil on November 29 and sailed to the site of modern-day Rio de Janeiro, where he

Below: An old print of one of Magellan's ships, the Victoria. The Victoria was the only one of the five ships of his fleet to return to Spain, having taken three years to sail around the world.

gave his crew a two-week vacation. Cartagena used it to conspire with de Coca, but again the mutiny failed, and Magellan put both Cartagena and de Coca under arrest. Magellan took a page from Bishop Fonseca's book and placed his cousin, Alvaro de Mezquita, in command of the *San Antonio*.

The Moluccas' Fleet departed Rio harbor on December 26, 1519, and sailed south. On January 11, 1520, it reached the estuary of the Plate River. Four of the ships remained there for three weeks, while the *Santiago* sailed up the Plate to see if it was the strait they sought. When he found that the Plate was indeed a river and not a strait, Magellan continued south on February 2.

AKG, London

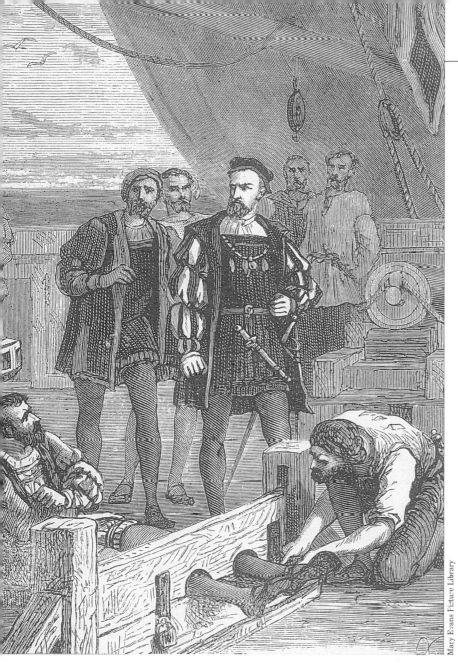

Mutineers took over the *San Antonio*, the *Concepción*, and the *Victoria* on April 2. Quesada announced that the mutineers would follow Magellan only if he took them back to Spain.

QUELLING A MUTINY

Magellan sent some loyal sailors, including Espinosa, to sneak on board the *Victoria*. Espinosa cut Mendoza's throat, and the sailors regained control of the vessel. Quesada attempted to sail away in the *Concepción,* but Magellan fired at the ship, and Quesada surrendered. Magellan then tried Quesada for mutiny and executed him.

In May Magellan sent the *Santiago* south to look for the strait. She sailed about 70 miles (110 km) south, then ran aground off Rio Santa Cruz and had to be abandoned. Magellan decided to spend the rest of the winter at Rio Santa Cruz.

DISCOVERY OF THE STRAIT

The voyage in search of a strait was resumed on October 18, 1520. Three days later Magellan's ships sighted a cape,

Left: Magellan punishes the mutinous Cartagena by putting him in the stocks.

Mary Evans Picture Library

On March 31 Magellan arrived at San Julian. With the southern hemisphere's summer near its end, he decided to winter here. This desolate bay by the great plains of Patagonia was to be home to the fleet for five months.

The decision to stay was opposed by Cartagena, Mendoza, and Quesada, and many of the sailors were also unhappy.

While wintering in San Julian, Magellan named the surrounding area "Patagonia" (right), which means "Land of big feet," because the people of the region wore very large footgear.

Galen Rowell/Corbis

AKG, London

which they named Cape Virgins. Beyond it they found a bay, which proved to be the entrance to the long-sought strait to the Pacific that now bears Magellan's name. It took a month to navigate through the strait, with its maze of islands in the western sector.

In yet another mutiny Esteban Gómez took control of the *San Antonio* and sailed her back to Spain, while Magellan wasted time searching fruitlessly for the vessel. The remaining three vessels entered the Pacific on November 28, 1520. For most of December the fleet headed north until it reached about 30° South, where it began heading west.

CROSSING THE PACIFIC

The vast Pacific nearly defeated Magellan. Apart from a couple of coral atolls, the course he set missed all the big islands in the then uncharted ocean.

Above: In late October 1520 Magellan's ships finally found the strait leading to the Pacific. It proved to be a hazardous passage through many islands.

Magellan begged the sultan to name an enemy that the Europeans could go fight on his behalf. Humabon suggested Rajah Lapu Lapu, ruler of part of the nearby island of Mactan. Magellan agreed to lead an expedition against him, but it ended in disaster. On April 27, 1521, Lapu Lapu's forces, armed with poison-tipped arrows, drove Magellan's

In April 1521 Magellan had an audience with Humabon, sultan of Cebu Island in the Philippines (below).

The fleet had no fresh water or food for two months. The crews were reduced to eating leather, and scurvy set in.

The fleet eventually made landfall at Guam, where they spent three days revictualing before sailing on to Samar, an island in the Philippines. Magellan set up a camp on Homonhon Island, and a group of Filipinos arrived. Gifts were exchanged, and on April 7 Magellan met Sultan Humabon, ruler of Cebu Island.

Mary Evans Picture Library

RICHARD HAKLUYT

In 1580 the first English account of Jacques Cartier's voyages to the Gulf of St. Lawrence was published. It was translated by John Florio, an Anglo-Italian, and promoted by Richard Hakluyt, a young clergyman. Hakluyt made it his life's work to publish books that would encourage English sailors to explore the world. He concentrated his work on material about eastern North America and India.

In 1582 Hakluyt brought out his own book, *Divers Voyages Touching the Discoverie of America.* His greatest work, however, was *The Principall Navigations, Voiages, and Discoveries of the English Nation*, published in 1589. The book inspired the generation of English explorers who followed Hawkins and Drake, Raleigh and Jenkinson. When Hakluyt died in 1616, there was an English colony in North America, and English ships were a familiar sight around the globe.

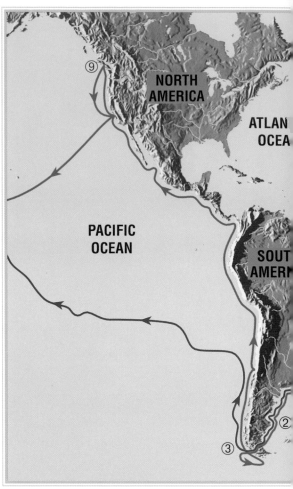

Mary Evans Picture Library

heavily outnumbered landing party into the sea. Magellan himself was killed attempting to cover his men's retreat.

When the Moluccas' Fleet sailed from Cebu, the *Concepción* proved unseaworthy and had to be abandoned. The remaining two ships, under the command of Juan del Cano, reached Tidore in the Spice Islands in November 1521. The *Victoria* and the *Trinidad* loaded up with spices, but the latter needed repairs. So the *Victoria,* under del Cano, sailed alone on December 21, 1521, crossed the Indian Ocean, rounded Africa, and reached Spain on September 6, 1522, with just 18 men.

Left: Magellan was killed in the Philippines while trying to protect his men. Del Cano took his ship, the Victoria, *back to Spain.*

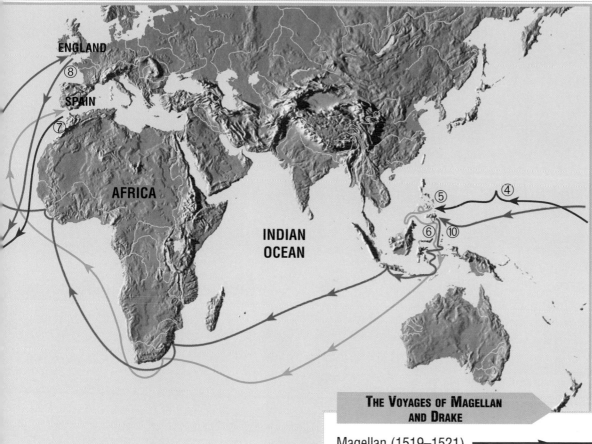

Left: A map of the routes taken by Magellan, del Cano, and Drake. Magellan was killed in the Philippines, but del Cano sailed on to complete the round trip of the globe. Some 50 years later Drake sailed around the world in the Golden Hind.

THE VOYAGES OF MAGELLAN AND DRAKE

Magellan (1519–1521) ———————▶

Del Cano (1521–1522) ———————▶

Drake (1577–1580) ———————▶

① After sailing from Spain in September 1519 with five ships and 250 men, Magellan reaches the River Plate estuary in January 1520.

② Magellan's fleet reaches San Julian in March 1520 and spends the winter there. Magellan puts down a mutiny, and the *Santiago* is wrecked.

③ Magellan's fleet discovers the strait leading to the Pacific Ocean. The *San Antonio* deserts and returns to Spain.

④ Magellan's remaining three ships reach Guam after almost 100 days out of sight of land and take fresh water and food on board.

⑤ Magellan reaches the Philippines in April 1521, where he is killed in a local war.

⑥ The two remaining vessels, under the command of Juan del Cano, arrive at Tidore in the Spice Islands and take on a cargo of spices.

⑦ Del Cano arrives back in Spain on the *Victoria* with the 18 surviving crew in September 1522.

⑧ Drake sails from Plymouth, England, in his flagship, the *Golden Hind*, with four other ships, December 1577.

⑨ After sailing through the Strait of Magellan, Drake sails up the west coast of the Americas, possibly reaching as far as Vancouver Island.

⑩ Drake reaches the Spice Islands in October 1579, before setting his course back to England around the Cape of Good Hope.

The repaired *Trinidad* tried to recross the Pacific, but easterly winds drove her back to Tidore, where a Portuguese squadron seized the ship. It was years before the last of the *Trinidad*'s crew returned to Spain from captivity in the Portuguese islands.

After navigating the *Victoria* halfway round the world back to Spain, Juan del Cano made another attempt to sail around the world. He left Seville in 1524 with a larger expedition that intended to follow Magellan's course. But the fleet was only halfway across the Pacific when he died aboard his ship in 1526.

SAILING THE STRAIT

The Strait of Magellan was an impractical route for regular sailings between the Spanish colonies in the Pacific and Spain itself. The strait was too far south, and it was cheaper to sail with gold and silver to Panama, carry them overland by pack train, and put them on ships for the voyage across the Atlantic Ocean. But for most Europeans the strait was the only route through to the Pacific.

Francis Drake planned to sail into the Pacific and raid Spanish colonies.

In the 1570s the strait attracted interest from England. At the time there was open warfare between the English and Spanish "beyond the line" of the Treaty of Tordesillas, although in Europe the two kingdoms were at peace. The riches of Peru and Bolivia traveled north in ships along the coast of South America to Panama. In the Caribbean the Spaniards had organized protection for their treasure fleets, while the Pacific was safe from English and French privateers because they had never reached that ocean. But this safety was not to last.

DRAKE SETS SAIL

In 1576 Francis Drake planned a voyage through the Strait of Magellan to the Pacific, intending to raid the Spanish colony of Peru and the shipping along the coast. The English queen, Elizabeth I, delayed giving permission to Drake's plans until July 1577, so it was not until December 1577 that Drake finally left Plymouth in his flagship, the *Golden Hind*, and four other small ships.

He sailed south along the coast of Africa to the Cape Verde Islands, where he captured two Portuguese carracks. He added one to his fleet and also found he had taken prisoner a Portuguese pilot, Nuño da Silva, who was very experienced in sailing in the southern hemisphere. Da Silva's help was invaluable once Drake's fleet reached South America.

Cordaiy Photo Library Ltd./Corbis

From San Julian Drake sailed with three ships to Cape Virgins and got through Magellan's strait in only 16 days. There he established that there was open sea beyond Tierra del Fuego, which meant that the island was not the tip of a great southern continent, as some people had believed.

However, he had not expected the fierce winter of the southern hemisphere. A terrible storm struck just after they entered the Pacific. One ship was never seen again, and the remaining two became separated. Drake continued the voyage in his ship, the *Golden Hind*, while the other returned to England.

PILLAGE AND PLUNDER

Drake now carried out with great gusto the mission of his voyage. The Spanish shipping in the Pacific was barely armed, and the harbors unguarded. Drake looted vessels—including a great treasure galleon—and plundered Spanish ports. Laden with booty, Drake carried on up the American coast hoping to find the western outlet of the Northwest Passage. He may have reached as far north as Vancouver Island before he turned back, putting in at what is now San Francisco for repairs.

A storm struck Drake's fleet in the Pacific, and one ship was never seen again.

In late July of 1579 Drake set off across the Pacific, reaching the Spice Islands in October. He took on a cargo of cloves and continued across the Indian Ocean, rounding the Cape of Good Hope in June 1580. He returned to Plymouth in September of that year.

Drake's voyage was spectacularly successful—with his plundered Spanish treasure he had achieved a 5,000 percent

Habes Lector candide fortiſs, ac inuictiſs Ducis Draeck ad Viuum ſmaginem qui toto terrarum orbe, duorum annorum, et menſium decem ſpatio, Zephyris fauen tibus circumducto, Angliam ſedes proprias, 4. Cal Octobr, anno â partu Virgi: nis 1580 reuiſit cum antea portu ſoluiſſet ſd. Decem: anni 1577.

Corbis/Bettmann

Above: Sir Francis Drake, who sailed into the Pacific in 1578 to plunder the Spanish colonies.

Left: A replica of his ship, the Golden Hind.

On June 18, 1578, Drake's fleet reached San Julian, where Magellan had wintered in 1520. Drake was confronted with a mutiny here. Drake believed that Thomas Doughty, a wealthy young nobleman, was the focus for the mutiny. He had Doughty tried and beheaded.

GERARDUS MERCATOR—A WORLD-CLASS MAPMAKER

Looking at a map on paper is misleading: the image is flat, but the area it portrays is curved. For most of us this is not a problem, but it presented serious difficulties to the early navigators.

The first geographer to offer a solution was Gerardus Mercator, who was born in Belgium in 1512. In order to be able to measure distances accurately on a flat map, it is necessary to adjust the scale in different areas. Mercator's map distorted the shape of the continents and islands both vertically and laterally. It also distorted the sizes of land masses. Greenland, for example, will look larger than South America on a Mercator-projection map, when in fact the reverse is true! But because the angles where lines of latitude and longitude meet are more accurate, navigators found his maps easier to use.

Below: Mercator's world map of 1569.

AKG, London

profit on his backers' investment—and he was the first mariner to take his own ship around the world.

THOMAS CAVENDISH
In 1586 a young English courtier, Thomas Cavendish, set out on the first voyage that was intended from the outset to be a voyage around the world.

Like Drake, he sailed through the Strait of Magellan and up the west coast of South America to raid Spain's Pacific colonies. He captured a galleon off the coast of California. He sailed back to England via the Philippines, the Strait of Lombok, and the Cape of Good Hope.

Cavendish was not simply seeking wealth. He gathered information about sailing in the Far East that was completely new to English navigators.

The Spice Islands, or Moluccas (right), were the lure for the early around-the-world sailors.

Chris Rainier/Corbis

Hulton Getty

A Dutch navigator, Olivier van Noort, also succeeded in circling the globe. There were also several failed attempts to follow in Magellan's wake, including one by the Arctic explorer John Davis.

Magellan had proved that the East Indies could be reached by sailing west.

Magellan, strictly speaking, never sailed around the world. Nor had he wanted to. But accidentally, he was the first European to get around the globe, since his visit to the Spice Islands in 1511 placed him east of the Philippine island where he met his death. He settled the dispute that Columbus had started 35 years before. The East Indies could be reached by sailing west. But since the Earth was as large as ancient geographers had calculated, many mariners who attempted the voyage in the 16th century did not survive it.

The young English courtier Thomas Cavendish (below) sailed around the world in Drake's wake in 1586.

SET INDEX